TI 00185 2924

W9-BMD-326

Highly Effective DISCARD
Networking

Meet the Right People and Get a Great Job

ORVILLE PIERSON

CAREER
PRESS
Franklin Lakes, NJ

15

Copyright © 2009 by Orville Pierson

HIGHLY EFFECTIVE NETWORKING
EDITED BY KATHRYN HENCHES
Cover design by Jeff Piasky
Printed in the U.S.A.

This publication is designed to provide accurate and authoritative information with regard to the subject matter covered. It is sold with the understanding that the publisher is not engaged in rendering legal, accounting, or other professional service. If legal advice or other expert assistance is required, the services of a competent professional person should be sought. (From a declaration of principles jointly adopted by a committee of the American Bar Association and a committee of publishers and associations.)

Except for the author's family, the characters in stories, examples, and the Orville's Journal sections are completely fictional, but represent the thoughts, words, and feelings of the many people that the author has assisted in job hunting over the years. Any resemblance to real people or real events is purely coincidental.

To order this title, please call toll-free 1-800-CAREER-1 (NJ and Canada: 201-848-0310) to order using VISA or MasterCard, or for further information on books from Career Press.

CAREER
PRESS
The Career Press, Inc., 3 Tice Road, PO Box 687,
Franklin Lakes, NJ 07417
www.careerpress.com

Library of Congress Cataloging-in-Publication Data

Pierson, Orville.
    Highly effective networking : meet the right people and get a great job / by Orville Pierson.
       p. cm.
    Includes index.
    ISBN 978-1-60163-050-6
    1. Job hunting. 2. Business networks. 3. Social networks. I. Title.

HF5382.7.P54 2009

650.14—dc22

*Dedicated to
Gail Watt,
my first writing coach.
Thanks, Gail.*

Acknowledgments

This book was made possible by the generosity of Lee Hecht Harrison (LHH), my current employer. I am particularly grateful to Steve Harrison, the second "H" in LHH, for his support through the years. I would also like to thank three of LHH's current top managers, Peter Alcide, Barbara Barra, and Kevin Gagan for their support of this project.

It is a privilege to have the opportunity to talk regularly with LHH's huge staff of career coaches. Although it's part of my job to "train" them, I learn at least as much from them as they do from me. Thank you, all.

And it's a privilege to lead LHH's Design Team in the creation of online and printed materials for career transition. I currently supervise the work of Susan Bassett, Richard Holt, and Larry Prendergast. But again, I learn a great deal from working with these outstanding instructional designers, content experts, and writers.

A number of people assisted me in the writing of this book by reading the manuscript at various stages of its development and offering some excellent comments and suggestions. Thank you David Haddad, Gita Haddad, Nancy Vescuso, Rob Saam, Bill Thomas, Jess Dods, Cori Ashworth, Salena Reynolds, and Delia Withey.

I am particularly grateful to my writing coach and friend, Peter Sugarman. He read the manuscript carefully and repeatedly providing comments that improved the book as well as my writing skills. He's an excellent writer, and if you're lucky, you may one day get the chance to read something written by him.

This book is in print because of my literary agent, Jeff Herman, and the great team at Career Press. Thank you, all.

My adult children both made significant contributions to this book, as they did to the last one. Sarah is an excellent networker and the inspiration for some parts of the book, including the Rachel character. Paul, an accomplished graphic designer, designed the interior of the last book and provided advice and assistance with this one. Both also provided content advice. Thank you.

Among all the people whose assistance I want to acknowledge, my wife Judy is by far the most important. She helped me organize the material. She assisted by reading the daggone manuscript repeatedly and making comments—even though she's heard this stuff from me for years and is probably a bit tired of it.

But the real point is this: it's in significant part because of her that I've become a person capable of writing a book that might be worth reading. Her deep commitment to personal and spiritual development has been a powerful support for decades, in writing books, and in life. Thank you, Ramala, for everything. It's a blessing to have you in my life.

Finally, I want to acknowledge the great teachers and saints who offer us guidance in everything in life and bring us closer to God every day. And I acknowledge God's grace, active in this book as it is in everything, everywhere, always. Thank you, Lord.

Contents

All experts agree that networking is an important part of job hunting. But there is much less agreement on the best way to do it. In this chapter, I'll tell you about my experience creating programs used by more than a million job hunters, and what I learned about networking while doing that. I'll also introduce you to my neighbor Ben and his experience networking for a job.

If you want to manage your job search project and make it effective, it might be smart to be systematic about your networking. You don't have to run out and buy a new computer, database software, and a stopwatch; but you don't want to just dabble either. It would help to think about it and plan it. Here's how highly effective networking fits into a highly effective job search.

You don't have to be a born schmoozer, a salesperson, an Old Boy, or a social butterfly to succeed in job-search networking. For 30 years, I've designed networking approaches that work for people who don't network very much and even for people who would rather not network at all. The first step is to eradicate some of the erroneous ideas that are found in some books and Websites.

Top experts define networking differently from the authors of some popular networking books. It's less complicated—and much less aggressive—than many people think. Whoever you are, you network nearly every day, usually without noticing that you're doing it. This chapter covers all of the basics: information exchange, commonalities, relationships, and communities. And how they'll help you find a job.

Everyone is an active or passive member of a number of different networks. Most people don't realize how many networks they have access to right now. Here's how to locate them, label them, and gauge their usefulness in your job search—and add them up into a Total Network that is a major asset in job hunting.

A highly effective job search doesn't happen by accident. Like any work project, it's the result of good planning and working smart. You're successful because you know how the job hunting game works and how to play it. When you create a Project Plan for your search, your networking quickly becomes more effective.

Which of your networks are personal rather than professional? This chapter is about how you can identify your personal networks and use them in job hunting. You'll also want to identify personal and professional communities that you may have access to, because networking inside a community can accelerate your search—and make networking more comfortable for all concerned.

Chapter Eight. Build Your Professional Networks

If you have more than a year or two of work experience, you are an active or passive member of one or more professional networks. If you are a recent college grad, you may not yet have any professional networks. If you're an executive, you may have a huge one. This chapter is about expanding and strengthening your professional networks, and using them in job hunting, no matter where you are starting.

Chapter Nine. Networking Tools and Advanced Strategies

If you want an extra edge, this is your chapter. Once you understand effective networking, you can take it to the next level by using some additional strategies and making the best use of social networking Websites, and other Internet, computer, and paper-and-pencil tools.

Chapter Ten. Moving From Networking to Interviews
and Job Offers

Well-planned networking is designed to move your job hunting from networking to interviewing to job offers. This chapter is about putting it all together—and when to stop networking and start interviewing.

I'm Orville Pierson. I'm a job search expert.

Networking is the most important part of job hunting.

It's also the place where most job hunters get stuck.

That's why I wrote this book.

Chapter One

Everybody Knows You Need to Network

Virtually all experts agree that networking is an essential part of job hunting, but there is much less agreement on the most effective way to do it.

There's no doubt that networking can help you conduct a better job search and find a better job—if you can find comfortable and effective ways to network. It looks to me like a lot of job hunters are not entirely comfortable with networking or not sure about the most effective ways to do it. Which is why I decided to write this book.

My name is Orville Pierson, and my job is helping people find jobs. I have spent most of my life doing that. I have worked privately with hundreds of individuals from the day they decided to find a new job until the day they accepted one. I have provided coaching and consulting for all kinds of people, ranging from recent college grads to senior executives. I have also worked with hundreds of people in groups, creating and teaching job hunting classes.

Throughout my career, nothing has made me happier at work than seeing people do effective job hunting and find great new jobs.

Since 1977, I have worked for five different career services firms. I am now a member of the U.S. corporate headquarters staff of Lee Hecht Harrison (LHH), a global consulting company with 240 offices around the world. We do executive coaching and leadership consulting, career management work with people who are employed, and career transition work with people who have lost their jobs in large downsizings.

That last one, career transition work, is also called outplacement. In case you're not familiar with it, here's how it works. When an employee of a large organization is let go in a downsizing, the organization often gives them severance pay and assistance in finding new employment. LHH provides that assistance. It's paid for by the organization, not the individual. Which is a good thing, because the services can cost thousands of dollars per person.

I have been with Lee Hecht Harrison since 1992, and through the years we have helped up to 100,000 people a year find new jobs in the United States alone. That work is done by career consultants in our nationwide network of offices. I lead an LHH design team that creates the programs, processes, books, Websites, and other tools used by our clients in career transition. I also train career coaches and write guidebooks for them.

In 1991, I developed a new process called Job Search Work Teams that has proven very useful to LHH's clients and is now being used in non-profits as well. I also designed a new way of teaching people how to find jobs—LHH calls it the AIM process—replacing an outdated 50-year-old curriculum that is still used by many in the career transition field.

My title is Senior Vice President, Corporate Director of Program Design, and Service Delivery. Journalists have sometimes called me an LHH "executive." That's not really correct, because I don't execute or manage much of anything. I design, counsel, advise, consult, write, and teach. And I love doing it.

With LHH and other career services firms, I have authored or co-authored dozens of books on job hunting for use by their private clients. Networking has been a central part of many of these books.

But the book you are holding is only the second book I have written that is available to the general public. And it's the first time I've written an entire book on networking—including everything, all in one place.

THE ADVANTAGES OF NETWORKING IN JOB SEARCH

It's clear to me that networking has great value in job search. I've heard that repeatedly from experienced LHH career consultants. And I've seen it myself hundreds of times. There are a couple of classic academic studies that demonstrate that the majority of job hunters find jobs by networking. I once also saw a report that said that people who find their jobs through networking are more likely to like their job and stay in it longer than people who find jobs using other methods.

But most of us in job search assistance don't need a study to tell us that kind of thing. It seems obvious, because people who network have more and better information than those who don't. So they have more choices and make better decisions.

Along the way to enabling people to find great jobs, networking has other benefits. It helps people collect the information they need to decide what kind of work they want to do. In the same way, it helps them decide *where* they want to do that work—in what units, departments, or areas, and for what kinds of employers.

It also helps them gather information on potential employers, so they can choose the particular employers best suited for them. It helps them survey what's going on in their profession and industry and what the "going rates" of compensation are, so they can better negotiate salary. And it's the single most common way that people meet the Decision Makers who offer them jobs.

All of this was true when I started in this field in 1977, and it is still true today. The Internet makes it easier to be more effective in networking, but it has not replaced networking. Even if you're part of that lucky minority that finds jobs through ads, postings, or head-hunters, information you gather through networking will help you make better decisions—and increase your chances of landing a really great job.

When the economy is good, networking is important. In tough times or tough job markets, networking is essential.

THE BEST WAY TO TEACH JOB SEARCH NETWORKING

Early in my career, I had problems teaching the networking part of job-hunting programs. I taught people how to do networking, but they didn't do it. So I taught it again, more carefully and more thoroughly. But they still didn't do it.

I didn't have that problem teaching resume writing, interviewing, salary negotiations, career direction, or any other part of the job-hunting curriculum. In other subjects, I provided the teaching and coaching, and my clients quickly performed very well. But in networking, they just didn't do what I wished they would. Their efforts were not very effective.

After a while, I realized that there were three reasons why my clients didn't behave as I hoped they would in their networking. First, they didn't believe that networking would work—or didn't believe it was a necessary part of effective search. Second, they had misconceptions about networking that I had failed to address. And third, they just plain weren't comfortable doing some of the things suggested by the books I was then using.

Through the years, I improved my teaching—and the books. When I began designing programs to teach networking, I went further. I looked for networking approaches people were more comfortable with. I went beyond the job-search books to study how networking is used in other parts of life. I used what I learned to make the process more understandable and more comfortable for job hunters.

Networking also became much better known. More and more people have heard of networking and know that it's important in job hunting. At the same time, the misconceptions have increased. There's more misguided advice on networking. More and more people do networking poorly. More and more, people on the receiving end of badly done networking calls are offended.

NETWORKING IN SALES VS. NETWORKING IN JOB SEARCH

When I began thinking about writing this book, I read a number of the most popular books on networking. Most were about succeeding in sales and business, but many also suggested that the same methods could be used in job hunting. I found a great deal of advice that might be useful in sales, but is not useful in job hunting. I also found a great deal of advice I completely disagreed with.

The popular general networking books are often directed to people who want to become master networkers so they can increase their power and influence and make more money in business. I'm sure that some of the advice given will help people do that. But I think that's completely different from networking to find a job.

And I think that much of what they're talking about—while it might be very effective in sales—is not actually networking at all.

All of those things led me to write this book especially for people who want to use networking in job hunting. If you also want to build a huge and powerful network, that's okay with me. (If you're unemployed, however, I do think it might be smart to find a job first.) But this book is about finding comfortable, honest, and effective ways to *use the network you already have* to find a great new job.

You'll find that some of what I have to say is plain old common sense, applied to job hunting. But I hope you'll also see how a well-planned, systematic approach helps in networking, just as it does in everything you do.

NETWORKING IN A SYSTEMATIC JOB SEARCH

I have long seen job hunting as a work project that needs to be planned and managed like any other work project.

In the job search project, your plan starts with a clear statement of what kind of work you want and a list of employers you'll pursue. And of course, it includes planning what you'll say to those particular employers—on your resume and elsewhere.

An effective job-hunting plan nearly always includes the use of networking. And of course, the networking will be more effective if you plan it than if you just muddle through. In the next chapter, I'll outline a systematic approach to job-search networking that I formulated from watching the most (and least) effective networkers. In following chapters, I'll explain it all in detail and even suggest what you might say at key points in the process.

This A-to-Z coverage of networking in job search may be more than you need. You may find a job before you do half of it. You may need only a few of the things that I have included in order to find a great new job. But I thought it would be best to give you the whole thing, just in case you needed it.

Of course, you don't need to learn every bit of it. Or even agree with all of it. Please just take the parts that will help you, then put the book down and get your job search moving.

As I explain things throughout the book,

I'll Put All the Important Points in a Large Font, Like This...

...so you can easily scan the main topics, skim any material you're familiar with, and find what you want if you come back to review it later in your job hunt.

One more thing: Before we move to Chapter Two and get started, I want to tell you about Ben and Jessie and the role they play in this book.

BEN AND JESSICA WILLIAMS

A couple of years ago, my neighbor Jessica Williams was job hunting. She and her husband Ben read a draft of my first book, *The Unwritten Rules of the Highly Effective Job Search*. The three of us discussed it, chapter by chapter.

Jessie used that book in her job search. I was her job hunting coach. She also networked with my wife, Judy. In the end, Jessie not only found a great new job, she also made a plan for the job after that and for her future career.

After Jessie got back to work, three other things happened. Judy and I became friends with Ben and Jessie. The two of them started using the Job Search Work Teams from my first book in their church jobs program. And things started to go south at Ben's employer.

Ben's company lost money for six months in a row, something that had never happened before. The company's Chief Executive Officer was fired. Ben quickly discovered that the new CEO had turned around three previous companies that were losing money. All three of these business successes included unhappy events for employees—major downsizings. In one case, 8,000 people were let go on the same day.

I figured I might be his career coach before long. I often do that for friends and relatives who are job hunting.

So, I wasn't surprised when Ben stopped by to discuss it with me. The first discussion led to more, and we brought in some other people, including Rachel, a friend of Jessie's who is a great networker.

I recorded those discussions in my author's journal. With the permission of all participants, I have included parts of those discussions in this book to provide some additional points of view. They're at the end of each chapter, and the first one begins on the next page.

ORVILLE'S JOURNAL

Ben's Job Goes Somewhere Else

"They sent my job to Canada," Ben said as he walked into my office. I had heard him chatting with Judy in the living room before he came downstairs to my office. "I was offended. Or maybe it was Alaska. I'm not even sure."

"You're out of work?" I asked.

"Next Friday," he said, sitting down in the rocking chair like he always does. "I never thought it would happen to me. I knew about Al the Ax when they made him president, but I figured I'd keep my head down and be okay. Will you be my official job hunting coach?"

"Sure. We talk about everything else. I don't know why we can't talk about your job search. You got severance?"

"Severance pay? You're going to charge me?" He looked shocked. He almost popped out of the chair.

I laughed. "No. Calm down. You can't afford my outrageous fees. I just wanted to know how soon you'd be feeling financially desperate."

"I'm not desperate. I've got a great coach." He said, adding, "And six months severance. The max."

"Six months? That's great. You could make a profit on this thing. I may have to charge you after all."

"Besides, I read your book. Again. I'm an easy client. I know practically everything. And I've got a job hunting team at my church. The one Jess and I started two years ago."

"Well, if you've got all that going for you, what do you need me for?"

"Insurance. I'm an engineer. I like to build in a large margin for error."

"You're not an engineer." I turned off my computer and walked over to the couch. "You're the manager of an engineering department. There's a 50- to 100-percent salary difference."

"See? You just proved how much I need a coach."

I sat down and picked up a pad and a pen. "What kind of work are you going to look for?"

"The same. Engineering. I mean engineering *management*."

"Good. And what's your target market? Are there enough..."

"Wait a minute" Ben interrupted. "I just came over to say hello and sign up. I'm really glad I made the team, but I'm not ready to start yet. Cut me some slack, coach. I'm out of shape."

I smiled. "I'm sorry Ben. I jumped the gun." I set the paper and pen down. "You want some tea? I've got jasmine green today. When do you want to get started?"

Ben laughed. "Sometimes you're like a daggone hound dog, Orville. You think someone's going on a job hunt and you're off across the fields tracking one down."

I've been called a lot of things, but this was the first time someone called me a hound dog. I sighed. There's an old Elvis song about that, I thought, "You're nothing but a hound dog, just a..." I couldn't remember the rest.

"I'll pass on the tea," Ben said, interrupting my musings. "But I accept the offer of help. I really appreciate it, Orville. And I'm glad I have a coach that's raring to go. I just need a little time to finish up at work and start planning my search."

"Yes, that's exactly right, and it's what any good career coach would suggest. You want to test drive my new book? After you get done at work, I mean."

"I don't know. Do I need it? I've got your other one pretty much memorized. I'm all about Highly Effective Job Search. What is it?"

"Job search networking."

Ben's face lit up. "Right! I forgot you were doing one on networking! I was going to sign up with Rachel for networking lessons. You know, Jessie's friend from the university."

"I never met her."

"She's a fund-raising whiz. A gazillion dollar woman. I'm not a great networker. But she sure is. Knows everyone. I can read your book?"

"I'd love it. I want your opinions on it. Maybe I could get Rachel to take a look, too. Then I'd have…"

"Two perspectives. Genius and dummy." Ben smiled.

"Well, I wasn't going to say it exactly like that."

"Ben, you want some coffee?" It was my lovely and thoughtful wife, Judy, in the doorway.

"No," Ben said, "Thanks. I've done my freeloading for the day. I got a free book and a career coach. I'm heading out. Thanks, Orville."

"Ben?"

"Yeah?"

"So you'll get started on a plan for your job search?"

"Yes, coach," he replied. Then to Judy, "He's really tough, isn't he?"

"Yes," she replied, "He pushes hard. He's always going for the big win."

Job Search Networking

Decide to network effectively.

Prepare for job hunting.

Talk to personal and professional contacts.

Land a new job.

| DECIDE | PREPARE | TALK | LAND |

Chapter Two

Systematic Job-Search Networking

In job-search networking, the one most important thing is to make everyone you talk to comfortable.

Why? If they're not comfortable, nothing will happen. At least nothing useful. If they're not comfortable, you're not comfortable. Then what do you have? An awkward conversation everyone wants to end as quickly as possible.

It doesn't go anywhere.

Some job hunters accidentally make their networking partners uncomfortable by doing things they themselves don't approve of. Unemployed job hunters sometimes start feeling a little desperate. Then they get some networking advice they don't really like, but they believe they have to do it anyway. If they act on it without thinking, it can lead to trouble.

Now and then, you may have to push the limits of your own comfort zone a bit, but that's completely different from behaving in ways you know to be objectionable. It's that objectionable stuff—such as, "I'm not really job hunting; I just need 30 minutes of your time."—that really makes everyone uncomfortable.

There are many reasons why people sometimes aren't comfortable being on the receiving end of a networking call with a job hunter.

We'll be taking a look at the most common ones. And I'll suggest some language you can use to head off problems and move the conversation in a useful direction. My goal is to help you to find effective networking approaches that are comfortable for you—and everyone else.

What I want you to know right now is that the comfort of your networking partners is very much under your control. So is the success of your whole networking effort.

There are many things in job hunting that you cannot control. You can't make anyone interview you. You can and should work to influence their decision of who to hire, but you can't control it. You can't stop them from hiring their cousin instead of you. And you can't control the condition of the job markets. Whether you like it or not, hiring will happen faster in some job markets and slower in others.

But here's the good news: You can control networking. This is the part of job hunting where you're completely in charge.

You can make the right choices about who to talk to and when to talk to them. You can make your networking partners comfortable. You can collect important information, including inside information that gives you an edge. And you can get your name—and yourself—in front of the right Decision Makers in the right way: with integrity.

When you do those things effectively and persistently, you will find a good new job. Even if you don't do them really well, it will work—provided only that you stay with it. As you'll see, it's a numbers game. No matter how strong a candidate you are, you will probably need to have a lot of conversations.

You may sometimes feel discouraged. But remember, you only need one good job offer. And networking is the way most people get that one good offer. Sometimes they even get two or three good offers.

Not all of your networking conversations will succeed in moving your job search forward. There's a learning process here, just as there is with any new project. As you work on your networking, you'll get better at it.

You *will* need to work on it. At the beginning of a job search, many job hunters believe that they won't need to network. Or that they won't be able to do it. Or that it will be a highly unpleasant experience. So they begin their job hunting by doing everything but networking.

Some do find jobs using the Internet or recruiters, and I'm always happy to see people succeed, no matter how they do it. The majority sooner or later get started on their networking, sometimes after wasting many weeks of time that could have been productive if they'd started networking when they started everything else.

Once they get started, people *do* learn how to network. It's not an exaggeration to say that hundreds of thousands of people find jobs that way every year—some by accident, and some because they planned it. In every career services firm in which I have ever worked, the majority of job hunters found jobs by networking. In the end, they find their own best ways of doing it. Many end up enjoying it.

You might enjoy it too. In fact, it's perfectly okay with me if you enjoy every single networking conversation. I don't think you need to suffer to find a job. You might have fun. And you might learn something too.

I often have successful job hunters tell me that they learned things along the way, met some great new people, and helped others as much as others helped them—or more. So it's entirely possible for effective job search networking to have some perfectly lovely side effects—in addition to getting you into a great new job.

My intention with this book is to help you become as effective as possible as quickly as possible. With job hunting, like everything else in life, there's a learning curve. I'm hoping to tell you some things that will get you into a better job faster.

HIGHLY EFFECTIVE NETWORKING

I started this chapter with the importance of everyone being comfortable because I think it's the first step to effectiveness in job-search networking. Of course, it's not the only step. There is an entire networking process (outlined in the pages that follow) from deciding to network to landing a great new job.

Networking is something most of us use all the time, usually without thinking about it. It's how we find a doctor or decide what movie to see or get information on how to best take care of a cold. We don't usually call it networking. We call it "asking around" or just plain "talking to people."

Job hunting is a bigger project than finding a new doctor or picking a movie, so job search networking needs to be handled in a much more systematic way—just as you would handle any important work project. This means understanding your goals, doing some preparation, and having a reasonably structured approach. Let's start with the goals, then spend the rest of the chapter on the elements of a proven, systematic approach to job-search networking.

The Four Goals of Networking

1. **Get the word out.**
2. **Gather information.**
3. **Meet insiders at targeted organizations.**
4. **Get in touch with Decision Makers.**

The ultimate goal, of course, is a great new job. But effective networking is *not* mainly about looking for job openings. If a networking contact can tell you about an appropriate opening, that's great. It can and does happen. But where networking really excels is putting you in touch with Decision Makers *before* the job opening happens.

This proactive approach is something I'll explain more as we go. For now, suffice it to say that networking is mostly about becoming a candidate for jobs that are not yet announced. You do that by making yourself known to Decision Makers who have the authority and budget to hire people in the job title you want. In other words, you talk to your next boss and let them know you're interested in their next opening.

Do that at enough different places and the odds of one of them having an opening next week are pretty good. The more of them you talk to, the better your odds become. But it's not about sending them resumes. It needs to be the right kind of contact, which is usually networking.

The key is contacting them before the opening is published, and usually before the job is even open. After all, smart Decision Makers prefer not to wait until they're short-handed and desperate before they locate candidates. They know they have turnover. They keep their eyes open for candidates.

There's nothing mysterious about any of this. Most experts agree that more than 50 percent of jobs change hands this way. Some of us say it's more like 75 percent. At Lee Hecht Harrison, we have seen thousands and thousands of people get jobs like this, every year for more than 30 years.

Some people—25 to 50 percent, depending on which expert you believe—do indeed find jobs by responding to Internet postings or being connected to job openings by recruiters. Even if you're part of that lucky minority, networking will help you make better decisions as well as help you interview and negotiate salary more effectively.

So use recruiters and the Internet. And network while you're doing that.

Goal # 1:
Get the Word Out About Your Search and Yourself

The first and easiest goal of your networking is to let people know that you're looking.

Sometimes job hunters feel desperate about finding a job. Meanwhile, in the same job market, some employers are feeling equally desperate about finding good candidates. Of course, it's not necessary for anyone to feel desperate, but there's no system, no grand plan, for getting job hunters connected with employers. They find each other however they can. It's all a big game, this employment cycle—a constant dance.

If you're a job hunter, your first goal is to get in the game: let people know that you're available for employment. In doing that, of course, it's important to say what kind of employment you're available for and why you're a strong candidate for that kind of work.

The more people who know you're job hunting and exactly what you're looking for, the more likely it is that someone will put you together with the right employer. When this kind of matchmaking is done well, everyone benefits and each party is grateful to the other two.

So getting the word out about what you have to offer and your availability is an important networking goal. Please notice that it's easy to combine this with gathering information. The two usually fit nicely into the same conversation.

The more people you get this message to, the better and more quickly your job search goes. If you are currently employed, you may need to be careful about how broadly and loudly you spread the word. If you are unemployed, you certainly do not. Tell everyone.

Goal # 2:

Gather the Information You Need

The second goal of your networking is gathering information. You may need to do some of this before you broadly spread the word about your search, in order to clarify your core message about yourself. Once under way, most job hunters get the word out and gather information at the same time.

Exactly what information you need to gather depends on your circumstances. The most pressing information need for someone considering a career change might be information on professions and specific jobs and careers, so they can decide what direction they want their career to take. That kind of information might also be the first step for a recent liberal arts graduate.

For an experienced Chief Financial Officer who wants to continue as a CFO, information on industries might be most important, because senior financial managers are not limited to the last industry in which they worked. That same person might also want to know what's happening in their profession—what trends are hot, what top CFOs have done to become top CFOs, and what are the latest and greatest developments in IT, compliance, management, and accounting. This kind of information will help locate the right organization and the right opportunity. It will also help win the job, because well-informed people interview better.

For anyone, information about particular organizations is important. After all, where you work is just as important as what you do. It determines how long your commute is, what you get paid, what your future prospects are, and how happy you'll be going there every day. It's not just about the organization's policies, it's also about the culture—how people do things and how they treat each other. Locating specific organizations that fit with who you are and where you want your career to go is at the heart of proactive and highly effective job hunting.

Networking is also the very best way to get up-to-date and accurate salary information. You can find some on the Internet, and sometimes it's good. But all too often, it's government surveys that cover only a small number of the more common job titles. Or it's not company-specific. Or it's anecdotal and you're not sure about the reliability of the source. So for private sector jobs, networking is nearly always the best way to get the compensation information that will allow you to evaluate offers and effectively negotiate them.

Goal # 3:

Meet Insiders at Places You'd Like to Work

Although you want to talk to everyone, talking to people currently employed in places where you want to work is particularly useful. They can give you the information you need in order to decide whether you want to work there. They can provide information about specific jobs. And they can even introduce you to the Decision Maker, the person who could be your next boss.

I'd actually prefer that you talk to Insiders at (or below) your own level and in your preferred area before you talk to the Decision Maker. Why? Because the information you collect in those internal conversations will guide you in what to say—and not say—when you later talk to the boss.

Sometimes job hunters want to jump immediately to the fourth goal, talking to the Decision Maker. But in this project, like many projects, doing the steps in the right order can make you more effective. Whenever you can, talk to insiders at your targeted organizations—before moving up to the Decision Maker.

Goal #4:

Get in Touch With Decision Makers

The ultimate goal of networking in your job hunt, of course, is to meet and talk to the Decision Maker, the person who could actually hire you. As I mentioned, you will most likely talk to that person before there is a job opening. So the first conversation is not an interview, it's an informal conversation. It might be over lunch. But more likely, it's on the phone for a few minutes or standing in a hallway, saying hello.

It's important to let the Decision Maker know you exist, and that you are qualified, available, and definitely interested. Doing this in person or on the phone makes you a real person, not just a resume, and people hire people, not resumes. If you make a good first impression, that's an important step to getting on the short list.

If you are introduced to the Decision Maker by someone they know and trust, that's even better. Networking is the way most successful candidates first meet their next boss.

When you use networking to gather information, get the word out, meet insiders, and get in touch with Decision Makers, you are moving systematically, step-by-step toward a new job. I'm here to teach you that kind of networking system, in the four steps that are listed below. It's a networking system designed especially for use in job hunting, based on principles tested with thousands of job hunters.

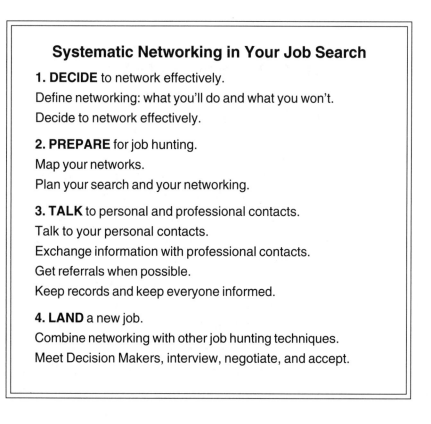

Systematic Networking in Your Job Search

1. DECIDE to network effectively.
Define networking: what you'll do and what you won't.
Decide to network effectively.

2. PREPARE for job hunting.
Map your networks.
Plan your search and your networking.

3. TALK to personal and professional contacts.
Talk to your personal contacts.
Exchange information with professional contacts.
Get referrals when possible.
Keep records and keep everyone informed.

4. LAND a new job.
Combine networking with other job hunting techniques.
Meet Decision Makers, interview, negotiate, and accept.

Sometimes people ask why I put "Decide" as the first step in the sequence. I do that because many people don't decide to network. They try the Internet; they mail out resumes; they call recruiters. Finally, they half-heartedly start networking only when nothing else works. When they back into it like that, they usually don't plan it. Then it's more about muddling through than being effective.

Networking is always part of an effective job search. That's true even when the Internet, resume mailings, and recruiters all work for you. It's even more important when those things don't work for you. So it makes sense to include networking in your search from the very beginning.

---

1. DECIDE to network effectively

Define networking: what you'll do and what you won't.
Decide to network effectively.

As someone reading a book on the topic right now, maybe you have already decided to network effectively. If so, congratulations! You're on the right track! If you're still on the fence, I hope you'll stay with the book and give me the chance to show you why it might be a good idea and how you can succeed at it.

Sometimes people who have decided to network postpone getting started because they dread the thought of doing it. When I talk to these people, I usually find that they have some serious misconception about networking. Or at least that they don't see it the way I do.

This is why I wrote Chapter 3 on networking myths. I'm hoping to get some of the misconceptions out of the way—at least the worst ones. Then, in Chapter 4, I'll explain exactly how I see networking, based on definitions by social scientists, as well as my own experience in working with job hunters. Networking isn't that difficult. We do it all the time. What's important is to adapt authentic networking to job hunting.

Once you've made your decision to proceed with systematic and effective networking, the next step is preparing to do that.

---

2. PREPARE for job hunting

Map your networks.

Plan your search and your networking.

In Chapter Five, we'll talk about how to map all of your networks. Everyone is a member of multiple networks. You may find that you are a member of more networks than you thought. And you may find that your total network is bigger than you think. About 90 percent of the people that I've worked with through the course of my career have initially underestimated the size of their total network, the one they can use in job hunting—and usually underestimated it by quite a lot.

Whether you're part of that 90 percent or not, it's important that you see exactly which networks you are part of right now—and the range of potential contacts you have in each of them. We'll also look at how each of these various types of networks can be useful in your job search.

In Chapter Five, you'll also start to see who you'll talk to and for what purposes. Before you finish that chapter, I hope you'll see that your Total Network, the sum of all your networks, is so big that you will need to be selective about who you contact and who you don't.

Make a Project Plan for Your Search

Start with Professional Objective, Target Market, and Core Message. Make a Target List.

The first part of your Project Plan, your Professional Objective, is a brief statement of what kind of work you want to do. It defines what profession you're in and states your objective for your next step in that profession. (For more information, see Chapter Six).

You do not need to completely define your Professional Objective before you begin your job search. In fact, networking is a very useful tool for defining and refining your Professional Objective. This use of networking is particularly important for recent college grads and for people making significant career changes.

On the other hand, the more clearly you can define your Professional Objective, the more effective your job search becomes. Without any Professional Objective at all, you are just another person looking for a job.

Your Professional Objective defines the goal of your job search. It also tells potential employers—your Target Market—what category of jobs you're interested in. It focuses your search.

The second part of your job hunting Project Plan involves defining your Target Market. Here, you specify the kind of organizations where you would most like to work. This definition is then translated into an actual Target List of potential employers. This list is very important, because it focuses your efforts, allows you to be proactive, and increases the odds that you will end up working for an organization you really like. In fact, I believe that having a Target List on paper is just as important as having a resume.

The third part of your Project Plan is your Core Message. Many job hunters believe that the first step in job hunting is writing a resume. Actually, you will write a much better resume once you've given some thought to exactly who your readers will be. A good resume tells your readers, the Decision Makers in your Target Market, why you are a good candidate for the jobs suggested by your Professional Objective. The same Core Message that makes for a great resume is also at the heart of successful interviewing.

We'll talk more about the Project Plan and how to create one in Chapter Six.

INFORMATION NEEDS AND NETWORKING

As you work on those three parts of your Project Plan, you will begin to see where your information needs are. Do you need information to make the best choices on Professional Objective? Do you already know which organizations you want on your Target List, or do you need more information to create that list?

All job hunters need to gather as much information as possible on each organization on their Target List. Choosing the company you want to work for is a very important decision, and one that you don't want to make in a vacuum. Information on what employers are looking for—what they need and what they want to avoid—is very useful in creating your Core Message. This includes information on specific Decision Makers: who they are, what their needs and preferences are, and how they make their hiring decisions.

Some of the information you need is waiting for you right now on the Internet. Not just information about job openings, but also information about potential employers. But, of course, the very best source for this information is networking. It's through networking that you get the most up-to-date information and inside information not available elsewhere.

Once you've mapped your networks, made a plan, and defined your information needs, you're ready to start talking to people.

But I want to make sure that you're not out talking to a lot of people until you've done some planning. Sometimes people rush out and start networking in an unplanned way. This is much less effective, and it can actually do harm. It can take your search backward by creating incorrect impressions that you later have to change. And it can just plain waste a lot of people's time, including yours.

So, although you want to talk to a lot of people in your job search, it's usually smart to limit your contacts to just a few trusted friends until you get your Project Plan, Target List, and resume completed—or at least off to a good start.

---

3. TALK to personal and professional contacts

Talk to your personal contacts.
Get referrals when possible.
Exchange information with professional contacts.
Keep records and keep everyone informed.

When your preparation is far enough along, you're ready to talk to your personal contacts. Your Project Plan doesn't have to be perfect, just good enough to get started. Your Target List doesn't have to be finished either, but you need to have enough organizations on it to show people what kinds of employers you're thinking about.

Then you'll talk to a broader range of personal contacts. I'd suggest talking to the easiest ones first, the people you know best and are completely comfortable with. If you know the questions to ask, this group can provide information that will help get your search moving. They will help take you to the next level—a more polished Project Plan and a more complete Target List. (We'll talk more about how to do this in Chapter Seven.)

You will also see how and when you can best ask your initial contacts to refer you to other people. It's important that everyone is comfortable in this referral process, so it's important to do it at the right time and in the right way.

Suppose for example that I'm networking with you and you mention your friend Sam, who works at an organization I'm interested in. Of course, I'd like to meet him. But only if you believe that Sam and I will enjoy meeting each other. If we do and if we're good resources for each other—and maybe even like each other—then Sam and I are both happy. It's a win for everyone. Sam and I are both grateful to you.

On the other hand, if you were reluctant to introduce me to Sam and I pressed you to do so anyway, I frankly think I would be asking for trouble.

I mention this because while referrals are important in job search networking, how you ask for them and how you make arrangements is even more important. (More about this in Chapter Seven.)

As you talk to your personal contacts, you are showing them your Target List. The Target List is the single best topic of conversation in early networking meetings. It's an easy, pleasant, non-threatening topic of discussion. It can be highly productive because it can generate exactly the kind of information you need on organizations, their needs, and people who work there, including Decision Makers.

Sooner or later, conversations with personal contacts lead to actual introductions to people currently employed inside of your targeted organizations. Networking is quite different in this phase. You are now talking to professional contacts and building your professional network. You are no longer talking about your Target List. Now you're talking exclusively about the organization you're inside of. All of this is the subject of Chapter Eight.

In networking with professional contacts, the ideal first contact is someone currently in a job similar to the one you're looking for, someone who would be a peer if you worked there. This person is not only an excellent information source, they're also a potential ambassador for you.

For managers, executives, and other people who are looking for a one-of-a-kind job, the situation is a bit different. If you're going for a job title with a single incumbent, naturally you don't want to convey the impression that you're out to take their job. (More about this in Chapter Eight.)

Using the Internet in Your Search

Job boards work for some people.

No Website can do your networking for you.

Social networking sites can make your networking easier—if you know how.

In Chapter Nine, we'll talk about social networking Websites, the ones that are an outgrowth of old originals like Friendster and Facebook. Because there are an increasing number of sites that are designed for career use, you might wonder why I'm saving this topic until Chapter Nine. Here's why.

When the Internet first got started, many people said that the job boards—like Monster and the thousands of others that have sprung up—would revolutionize the hiring process. Job hunting would be easy, they said, just a few clicks and you'd have a job. There would be so many listings that anyone could get hired faster than ever before.

But it didn't happen.

The job boards have automated the formal application process, and that's a good thing. People do find jobs that way, and you should definitely include the job boards in your search. But the formal application process has never been the way *most* people find jobs and it still isn't. As always, most people find jobs using informal methods—in other words, by networking.

The same thing happened with social networking sites. When these Web 2.0 sites started moving toward work and career with the advent of LinkedIn, some people said that they'd revolutionize job-search networking. Just a few clicks and the word's out on the network, reaching tens of thousands of people in an instant, they said. Then you'd be shortly shaking hands with Mr. Bigshot or Madam President, and you'd have a job.

But that's not happening either.

The Internet—including job boards and social networking sites—is an extraordinary job-hunting tool, but not always in the ways that people think. And only for those who know how to use it.

Social networking sites can be enormously helpful in networking for a job, but only if you're good at networking. Many Websites are powerful job-hunting tools, but they won't do the job for you. You need to use the tools in the right way at the right time in your search. So we'll start with highly effective networking, then later I'll talk about using Internet tools as part of that.

In Chapter Nine, we'll also go beyond the Internet to look at additional ways to make your networking more effective. Like how to use software tools, connect with existing groups, and cover multiple cities. Then we'll move on to actually landing your new job, and what happens when you do that by networking.

---

4. LAND a new job

Combine networking with other job hunting techniques.
Meet Decision Makers, interview, negotiate, and accept.

The last step is not really networking at all. The first part is about combining networking with the other six job search techniques: staffing firms, responding to job ads and postings, completing applications, using direct mail, cold calling, and walking in. You'll find this in Chapter Nine.

Then, in Chapter Ten, we'll talk about going beyond all of the job-search techniques in order to wrap up a new position. When you get to this endgame through networking, the interviewing and ne-gotiating processes are easier.

Let's summarize the whole thing right now, all four steps. The majority of job hunters find new jobs through networking. When you do this, you typically meet the Decision Maker before there is a job opening. Later, when a job opens up, you have the inside track. You have an interview with a Decision Maker that you already met informally. This makes for a friendlier—and easier—interview.

If your introduction to the Decision Maker was through a person they like and trust, that's even better. In that case, the Decision Maker may be predisposed in your favor before the interview begins. This, of course, makes it easier to succeed in both interviewing and salary negotiations. You've picked up information in your networking that can be used in the job-hunting endgame. Then you start work in an organization you already know quite a bit about, one where you've already met some people.

This completes the quick tour through the entire book. If there are things you don't understand or you're not sure you agree with, I hope you'll stay with me and give me a chance to explain it more carefully and thoroughly in the appropriate chapter.

As soon as you take a look at my journal entry on Ben's reaction to this chapter—and his wife's objections to it—we'll get going with the chapter on the myths, misunderstanding, and dumb ideas that sometimes interfere with effective networking.

ORVILLE'S JOURNAL

Ben and I Don't Discuss Chapter Two

I was sitting with Ben on the Williams' patio when his wife Jessie stepped out of their house to ask, "Are you going to barbeque today?"

Then, noticing me, she added, "Oh it's job hunting. Hi Orville. I don't know why anyone needs two job hunting books. I did just fine with your last one. That 'Highly Effective Job Search' book."

Jessie is like that. She doesn't waste time. You always know what's on her mind.

"Jess, just because Orville is here doesn't mean that it's job hunting. We're always..."

"It's job hunting," I put in. "Chapter Two, Systematic Networking."

"Yes, I know. Ben let me read it. Is that okay? Your first book was great, Orville. I read it and I found a job. But why does the world need a whole book about networking? You talk to people. You find a job. What's the big deal?" Jessie moved right along. Sometimes you needed a Speed Listening course to keep up with her.

"I'm happy you're reading it," I said, "and I'm interested in your comments."

"Maybe networking is easy for you," Ben said, "but you're always hanging out with Rachel. She's a networking genius. Not that you're not, Orville," he added, glancing at me.

"Yes, she's good, but she didn't help with my last search. I hadn't met her then. I talked to my friends. I met some people. I got a job. What's the big deal?"

You did a great job on your last job search, Jessie," I said, "but networking comes easy for you. It's not so easy for most people."

"Yes, like me for instance," Ben said. "I don't know enough people. I don't know the right people. I don't know where to start and I don't know what to say." He smiled. "Once I get those four taken care of, maybe it will be easy for me too."

"Orville can't tell you what to say."

"Well, I hope someone can, because I don't have a clue." He picked up an imaginary phone. "'Hello, this is Ben. I just got canned. Do you know of any jobs for engineers? I mean for managers?'

Jessie gave him a look. "You know better than that, Ben Williams. You helped me figure it out more than once when I was looking."

"Okay, that's true. I can do better than that. But I'm an engineer, not a salesman, I don't have a clue what to say." He saw me giving him a look.

"Okay, okay, an engineering *manager*. A manufacturing manager, maybe. But I still don't know what to say in networking. Or where to start."

"What did you think of Chapter Two, Ben?" I asked.

"I liked that you have a system, a way to proceed. It makes sense."

"Good," I replied, "Then we're off to a good start."

"Maybe Rachel can tell me what to say. She does a lot of networking."

"Who is this Rachel?" I asked.

"Director of Corporate and Foundation Giving for Walcott University," Jessie said, "and very smart."

"She did class gifts at State before she moved to Walcott," Ben added. "That's how she got to know practically everyone. She's a great networker."

"Maybe we could invite her to join us next time," I said. "I'm sure she'll have some good suggestions. And I can give you some too. Networking in job hunting is sometimes very different from other networking."

Jessie smiled. "That's a great idea, Orville. I'll invite her."

"Can we get back to work, Ben?"

"Yes, Coach. I was saying that I like Chapter Two because you're systematic about networking. When Jess did it, it was like she said, she just did it. That was good, but she's kinda random. I saw her find a job by networking, but I never really understood how she did it."

"I admit to not being systematic," Jessie volunteered, "I'm not good at systematic. That's why I married you, hon, so there'd be some systematic in my life."

"You really did very well with it, Jess," I said. "You worked with both personal and professional contacts. You found a good job."

"It probably would have gone faster if I had planned it better," she said. "Are you going to barbeque today?"

"Yes," Ben replied, "Orville, are you having dinner with us?"

"Thanks Ben," I said, "but I've got a dinner date with Judy tonight. Why don't we plan for the three of us to get together as soon as we can make arrangements with Rachel?"

"That's good," said Jessie, "and maybe we can talk about a couple chapters of your book."

"Well, we won't have to talk about the Decide part of Decide-Prepare-Talk-Land." Ben said. "I've decided. I've decided to network. I've decided to do what my coach says. And to listen to Rachel too."

"What about me?" Jessie asked. "Orville said I'm good at networking. And job hunting."

"Honey, I always listen to *you*."

Networking Myths

1	You Have To Know a Lot of People.
2	It's About Meeting Mr. Bigshot or Madam President.
3	Power Networking.
4	You Have to Be a Used Car Salesman.
5	Networking Is Information Interviewing.
6	Networking Groups Are the Only Place to Network.
7	It's About Making Lots of New Friends.

DECIDE	PREPARE	TALK	LAND

Chapter Three

Networking Myths, Misunderstandings, and Dumb Ideas

Once when my daughter was very young, her mother and I told her that we were going to take her to the zoo. We had hoped she'd be delighted. But instead, she looked worried. She didn't say anything.

That evening, when I was tucking her into bed, she finally spoke up.

"Daddy," she said in a small voice, "When we're at the zoo, will the lions eat me?"

"No, sweetheart," I replied. "The lions are in a big pen with high stone walls. They're on an island in the middle of a lake. They don't know how to swim across the water and they can't climb up the walls, so the people are very safe."

"Oh," she said, finally looking relaxed.

I have seen the same story play out with job hunters. You tell them they need to network, and they don't say anything. They just looked worried. They don't do anything.

Later, with luck, you find out what they're worried about. The root of the worries is usually a misunderstanding about networking. Once the misunderstanding is cleared up, the networking goes a lot better. That's not surprising. I wouldn't want to network either if I thought I was going to be eaten by lions.

SEVEN MYTHS

Before we start talking about what networking really is and how to best use it in job hunting, I thought it might be a good idea to get some of the most common misunderstandings out of the way. I have chosen the seven that I've heard most often. Whether you call them myths, misunderstandings, or just plain dumb ideas, it's all the same. We'll save time later if we get them out of the way now.

I'm taking the time to look at them because I have actually seen every single one of them put forward in at least one book—as fact, not as myth. They are repeated again and again, until people come to believe them. Then they interfere with effective job hunting.

Here they are:

Networking Myth #1:

You Have to Know a Lot of People

Some people have huge networks. You may have met some of them. I have.

I remember the first time I met someone who seemed to have an endless network. It was many years ago, when people used Rolodexes, those rotating racks that hold index cards. But this man was way beyond Rolodex. He had two desks in his office, one where he sat and one that was entirely filled with boxes of index cards. There must have been 5,000 cards, maybe more.

At one point in our conversation, he got up and walked to the cards. He flipped through some cards over in the corner. Then he looked at some in the middle. He pulled out a few here and there. Then he turned around and said, "I know seven people who could give you more information on that. You want their names?"

I had probably met others who had equally large networks. But this guy had taken the trouble to put a lot of information on cards.

Now, it's all on laptops and autodials, so you can't see by looking at how big someone's network is. Or at least you can't see by looking at their desk. But you can usually find out by talking to them.

The most effective professional salespeople often have large networks. It's one way that they help their customers—by having fast access to information and by introducing people to other people.

The same is true of executive recruiters. They make their living partly by having a large network. Maybe it's easier for them. After all, everyone wants to meet them.

And politicians. It's part of the job to connect with a lot of people.

For people like these, having a huge network is how they became hugely successful. They spend a lifetime building the size of their networks. They pay a lot of attention to it. They might even have an assistant or two, sending out thousands of holiday cards or birthday cards every year. They often enjoy large social events, and may have brief conversations with a hundred people in one evening.

Most of us are not like this. These master networkers are a tiny minority. Some of us are at the other end of the spectrum. Like me. When I go to a large party, I usually talk to only a half dozen people all evening. And I'd rather not go to a large party at all. I have an e-mail address book, but it wouldn't take you all day to read the list. I'm connected with a number of work colleagues and some friends on social networking Websites. But I don't have a database of contacts, and I never owned a PDA.

IT'S NOT ABOUT HAVING A HUGE NETWORK. IT'S ABOUT USING THE NETWORK YOU HAVE.

You don't have to be a master networker to find a new job. You don't have to be enthusiastic about networking to find a new job. You will probably meet some new people while networking for a job, but it doesn't need to be hundreds.

If you know a master networker or happen to meet one during your job search, that can be an advantage. Every now and then, I talk to a job hunter who has the good fortune to have a master networker for a friend. That lucky person might make a lot of their contacts through the master networker.

And here's the other thing: If you know three or four people with average networks, that's just as good as knowing one master networker.

At Lee Hecht Harrison, we have assisted more than a million people in job hunting. Practically none were master networkers. Most had average networks. Some had small networks. They learned how to use those networks, and they found jobs.

So the most important thing is not to have a big network. It's knowing how to use the network you already have. Actually, it's about knowing how to use your networks, with an "s," because everyone alive is a member of more than one network. You map your networks. You see where the best starting points are. Your best initial networking partners are always people you already know.

Networking Myth #2:

It's About Meeting Mr. Bigshot or Madam President

Sometimes when people talk about networking, they refer to "six degrees of separation." You may have heard of it. The idea is that you can reach out to anyone on the planet with a maximum of six networking introductions.

If, for example, you wanted to reach the president of the United States, you might start by talking to a friend who introduces you to the mayor. That's reaching across two degrees of separation, the friend and the mayor. Then the mayor introduces you to a state senator. The state senator introduces you to a member of Congress. The member of Congress introduces you to a member of the president's staff. And the staff member introduces you to the president. Bingo! You have reached the president in six moves, six degrees of separation.

Now I don't believe that you or I could actually do that. At least not unless we had a message that all six people found highly compelling. But I do think it's a useful theory that can be applied in practical ways in a job hunt.

When job hunters hear the six degrees of separation theory, they sometimes take it to mean that job-search networking is all about meeting some very important person. They think about meeting TV stars or movie stars. They think that the key to job-hunting success is meeting a U.S. senator, or maybe the president of France.

The fantasy goes like this: if only you can meet some very important bigshot, they will take care of everything for you. By networking, you manage to get two minutes with Mr. Bigshot or Madam President. You say something really, really clever. They are so impressed that they are momentarily speechless. Then, recovering, they whip out their cell phone and say "Let me make a phone call."

Presto! The perfect job is arranged for you.

It's a great fantasy. If you can actually do it, more power to you.

TALK TO THE DECISION MAKER, NOT A MOVIE STAR

But here's the reality. In 30 years of working with job hunters, I have never heard of this happening. Not even once. Mr. Bigshot or Madam President is no more likely to need to hire someone than anyone else. But more to the point, if you're an accountant who wants to work in manufacturing, why would you talk to a movie star? Or the president of France?

It would make a great deal more sense to talk to people in your field. Personally, I think you would be better off talking to two or three average people who work inside manufacturing organizations—

or a couple of accounting managers—than talking to the president of France.

To get a job, you need to talk to Decision Makers in your targeted organizations—the people who could be your next boss. Talking to your next boss's boss is also good. Going higher is not necessary.

Doing all six degrees of separation—a chain of six introductions—is not how job hunting usually works. The good stuff in job search usually happens at the second or third degree of separation. A friend of a friend. A guy who knows a guy who knows the boss—probably because he works for her.

If you can easily get through to Mr. Bigshot or Madam President, you should do it. Why not? But you certainly don't have to. And it's probably not a good idea to spend a lot of time trying.

Networking Myth #3:
Power Networking

There is a popular school of thought that says concentrated, intense, well-organized daily networking is the route to success in business and in life. According to this school of thought, it is important to belong to the Old Boy Network, to hobnob with the rich and powerful, and to have lots and lots of contacts and friends. If you weren't born into this, the theory goes, you should work hard to meet the right people so you can become a member of this exclusive club.

In this view, networking is sometimes seen as calling in markers and swapping favors, not just exchanging information. In order to accumulate power, you do a lot of favors for a lot of people. Then you have a network of people who are indebted to you. There are always people you can call in order to collect a return favor so you can make things happen and get things done.

Networking is sometimes also seen as having a lot of friends, including influential friends. So you might also do people favors as a way of becoming friends with them. Or you might go to a lot of social events to meet a lot of people and then work persistently to build relationships with some of them.

There are a number of books with "networking" in the title that suggest approaches like these. Those who think this way often put a great deal of energy into the process they call networking. They work very hard to increase the size of their network. They put a great deal of energy into network maintenance. It becomes a way of life. It's seen as a route to success, wealth, happiness, and achieving the American Dream.

JOB-SEARCH NETWORKING IS DIFFERENT

I'm not at all sure that all of this is really networking. I'm very sure, however, that this approach is not necessary in job hunting. Job search is more about using your existing network than it is about building a bigger and better one. Networking is about information exchange around shared interests. To be successful in job search, you don't have to be an Old Boy or even talk to one.

Job-search networking is usually more about community than power. If you make some new friends along the way, that's good. But the main point is how you talk to the friends you already have—and work with them to connect with and talk to some people you haven't yet met.

While networking, people can and do help other people for the common good—without expecting anything in return. If they also want to be rich, powerful, and achieve the American Dream, that's okay with me, too.

Networking Myth #4:

You Have to Be a Used Car Salesman

Some people think that networking is really sales. It's not. The two are completely different.

It is true that salespeople use networking. The most successful salespeople often have large networks. And some of them write books about networking. That can be a problem. They often write books that confuse networking with sales, or at least don't draw a careful boundary between the two.

If you have never worked in sales, you may not be aware of the wide range of sales jobs out there. At the top are experienced professional salespeople with years of experience. Some have been trained in sales by top corporations and excellent sales training consultants.

These sales pros behave like consultants. They work hard to understand your needs and problems and then help you find solutions. They usually have excellent interpersonal skills and high integrity. Unless you are responsible for buying something expensive for a business or other organization, you may never meet these people.

At the other end of the spectrum are the really tough sales jobs like selling used cars or door-to-door selling. In order to make a living, these salespeople usually need to be aggressive. Sometimes they go too far. Some of us have had bad experiences with them.

There are also part-time salespeople who mix selling into their social life. They sell to their friends and acquaintances. They want to meet lots of new people and maybe sell something to them as well. This kind of selling is sometimes called multilevel marketing—or network marketing—once again blurring the line between networking and sales.

Salespeople of all kinds tend to create their own definitions of networking. I usually do not agree with these definitions. I prefer the definitions used by sociologists. Networking is not about selling. It's about information exchange between people who share common interests. It was in use long before there was a job called salesperson.

It might be a good idea to do a little selling at your job interview. I hope you will use the consultative kind of sales, where you work to understand the employer's needs and explain how you can help them fill those needs.

But before you get to the interview, while you're networking, it's not about selling. It's not about making phone calls to total strangers. And it is absolutely not about being dishonest or pushy. It's about shared interests. It's about information exchange. It's about friendly conversations everyone is comfortable with.

Networking Myth #5:

Networking Is Information Interviewing

There is a job-hunting technique called information interviewing. It's an excellent technique for recent (or about-to-be) college grads who are not yet sure of career direction. It is also useful for job hunters considering major career change. I often recommend it for those two groups. However, I believe it is inappropriate for pretty much everyone else. In general, the higher your compensation, the less appropriate information interviewing is.

The technique works like this. You network to locate people with information about the kind of work you want to do. Ideally, you start with someone who currently holds the job title you would most like to have. You request an information interview with that person. You want to do this because you're considering a career in a kind of work you've never done before.

At the information interview, you ask questions about the job and how it's done. Ideally, you conduct the information interview in the workplace, so you can actually see how things are done. A discussion like this takes at least a half an hour. You could easily use an hour or more. With a little luck, you might be able to stay for an entire day and get a really good feeling for that job and how it's done.

As useful as it is for some people, information interviewing is not networking. If you are exploring a career you have never tried, you may locate the opportunity to do an information interview through your networking, but the two are different. In networking, you don't always need a lot of time, and you ask a broader range of questions.

When people believe that networking and information interviewing are the same thing, they think that they're supposed to do information interviews with everyone they talk to. Then they ask strangers for more time than is needed and sometimes even ask questions they already know the answer to. None of this is appropriate, even for the recent grad. And for an experienced manager or professional not planning a major career change, it's in the dumb idea category.

If this isn't obvious, imagine an unemployed Chief Financial Officer saying "I'd like to set up an information interview with you. I want to find out what it's like to be a CFO. And I'd like to get information on financial management."

An experienced CFO is an expert in financial management and might very well offer some advice on financial matters to others as they look for a new employment. The CFO, like everyone else, will certainly collect information as part of a job search. But when networking with professional contacts, they're likely to give as much information as they get. Using the term "information interview" is more likely to be a problem than a help.

Information interviewing is a more formal planned activity that takes some time to do effectively. Networking meetings are sometimes like that. But more commonly, they're informal and much easier. When you're networking effectively, you can sometimes make good progress in a brief conversation on the phone or standing in a hallway. So use information interviewing if and when you need it. But use networking throughout your job search.

Networking Myth #6:
Networking Groups Are the Only Place to Network

Organizations wishing to assist unemployed people sometimes sponsor networking groups. These are often held in churches, synagogues, and community centers. I think it's a great trend, because there are numerous ways unemployed people can assist each other in job hunting.

If you can find a group that has values similar to yours, one where you like the other participants, it might be good to join it. But if you cannot find one you like, I want you to know that they are not necessary to job-hunting success. And they are definitely not the only place you can network.

Networking is a person-to-person activity. You don't need a group of any kind to do it. But if the group is structured in the right way, and you are comfortable with its activities, it can be an opportunity to get more networking done more easily.

In case you decide to use one, I'd like to say a few words about how to get the most out of it. Some networking groups actually go far beyond networking to offer full-blown job-search assistance programs, complete with training sessions, career counselors, job banks, speakers, resume assistance, and other great features. Some of the larger ones offer separate programs for managers and executives. They usually meet regularly, something between once a week and once a month. And they're usually free of charge.

Most have a "networking" part of the meeting. As a job-search assistance program designer, I pay particular attention to how that part works. A common design is what I'd call a cocktail party design, only with no drinks. Participants are expected to circulate in a room full of people, introducing themselves to others and exchanging useful job-hunting information.

People who are extraverted and skilled at introducing themselves can have useful meetings with dozens of people in a short time. So it can be very efficient. However, if you're less extraverted, you might find that part of the meeting uncomfortable and unproductive. If you're new to the group and don't know anyone, this is actually not networking at all. It's what salespeople call "working the room."

Some job hunting networking groups add more structure to the basic design: formal introductions, speed networking methodology, or exchange of written information, for example. I think that structures like these can make the group more inclusive and more effective for everyone.

The Job Search Work Teams I described in *The Unwritten Rules of the Highly Effective Job Search* (McGraw-Hill, 2005) are ideal in this kind of group setting—and designed to support networking as well as the overall job-hunting process. Because these small teams meet weekly, you get to know the other members. Then real networking can take place. The team becomes your core network.

So, can you network at a networking group? Yes, absolutely.

Is it the best place to network? Sometimes.

Is it the only place where you can network? No. For some people, they work well. But sometimes people can't find one where they're comfortable. Even if they work very well for you, you will almost certainly need to network outside of the group as well as inside of it.

Should you go to one? Sure. If you can find one that sounds good, give it a try. And if you like it, stay with it.

Networking works best when you know people, so the longer you're with the same group, the better it will work. If you're a member of the church, synagogue, or other group sponsoring the networking group, that's ideal because you have an organizational connection with other members and may already know some of them. You're networking inside of a community. In that case, I strongly recommend going to the meetings.

Networking Myth #7:

It's About Making Lots of New Friends

If you want to make lots of new friends, I suppose that networking is a good way to get started with that.

But in job hunting, making lots of new friends is not the point. The point—along the way to getting a great new job—is collecting the information that will make your job search more rapidly effective. And getting your message out to enough people.

While you're doing this, you may indeed make a few new friends. Or professional acquaintances. But, in my opinion, this is a happy side effect and not what job-search networking is all about.

MOVING BEYOND THE MYTHS

These seven are not the only myths and misunderstandings about job-search networking, but they are among the most common. I took the time to go through them because I don't think you can fully commit to the networking process unless you know what it's not and what it is.

Another reason networking myths are important is this: some of your networking partners might believe these myths to be reality. You may need to help people see more clearly how networking works before they're comfortable networking with you.

If, for example, one of your networking partners believes they need to be well-placed or have a huge network, they might feel awkward or embarrassed that they are somehow not good enough. You may want to discuss the myths with them, so they see that networking is all about ordinary people talking with other ordinary people.

Now that we've discussed what networking is not, we'll move to the "what it is" part. In the next chapter, we'll talk about real networking and take a look at how it works, in job hunting and elsewhere.

But first, let's visit with Ben and Rachel.

ORVILLE'S JOURNAL

It's Good to Have Friends Like Rachel

"I've got eight contacts at my old company, six guys from college, and two that I used to work with, but one of them's in Egypt on a project. Sixteen total." Ben was addressing Rachel, and looking a little depressed.

Rachel smiled. "And they're all men with engineering degrees?"

"Yes."

"What about me?" Rachel asked, "And your wife?" she added, nodding toward Jessie, who was just entering the Williams' living room with a tray of coffee, tea, and cookies.

"Ben," I said, "It's not just about professional colleagues. It's about everyone you know."

"But I'm not going to bother everyone I know with my job search. And besides, most people don't know where to find engineering or management jobs."

Jessie set the tray on the coffee table. "Ben, this is networking. It's not about *what* they know, it's about *who* they know."

"Like me," Rachel added. "I work for a university. I know people in all departments, including engineering. And I know faculty members who consult with corporations."

Ben took two cookies off the tray. "Okay," he said, "I was thinking too small. But still, I'm not a power networker like Rachel. And I don't want to run around begging everyone to find me a job."

"I already thought of 11 people you could talk to," added Jessie.

"Ben," I said, "It's not about job openings. The openings happen later in the process. First you talk to people about organizations. It starts with information, not with jobs."

"Okay," Ben said, "I can get started with those 16 and see where it goes." He was hunched over the cookie tray, reaching for another cookie.

"Ben!" Rachel spoke sharply. "Why do you keep excluding me? And Jessie? We're trying to help. Jessie said she had 11 contacts for you. I might have some too. We're both part of your network."

"I can't just go around asking everyone for help." He took a pair of cookies and ate them together, like a sandwich.

"Benjamin Williams, if you don't stop..."

"Jessie, wait. Please." I interrupted her. It looked like we needed a coach. "Ben, you're not paying attention."

He looked up from the cookie tray.

"You've got two people who are part of your network who are volunteering to network with you, and you're turning them down."

He was sitting up straight now, looking from me to Jessie to Rachel.

"This is a team effort," I continued, looking for the right speech. What would Vince Lombardi say, I wondered. "You don't try to do everything by yourself at work. You're a team player. Nobody does anything important all by themselves any more. You're not Michelangelo, toiling alone in your studio. You're a job hunter. You need to shape up and sign on with your team."

He was staring at me. I held my breath. Then he looked at Rachel.

"You're right," he said. "I was excluding you. I apologize." He turned to Jessie. "Hon, I'm sorry. I was all wrapped up in worrying."

"Sometimes it *is* about asking for help," I was breathing again. We were back on track. "But only with friends, people like us who want to help. Mostly, it's just about talking to people. All kinds of people."

"Yes," said Rachel, "You've got to get over this idea about begging and bothering people. There's lots of people that will enjoy talking to you."

"Ben, I think you're going to be okay about talking to people once you get clear on what to say," I put in. "Can you see that your network is bigger than 16?"

"Yes," he said, slowly nibbling a cookie, "I've added a zero."

"After you read the book some more, I'm hoping that you'll add at least one more zero," I added.

"Sixteen hundred!" Ben exclaimed, taking two more cookies. "You've got to be kidding."

"I think you have that many," Rachel said, setting her coffee cup on the table, "and I need to say something about Rachel the power networker. That's nonsense. I'm not Wonder Woman."

"You're not?!" Jessie feigned amazement. "Then how did you bring in 21 million dollars for Walcott last year?"

"Okay, I'm good at fundraising, but there's no mystery in networking. When I started, I was a School of Social Work dropout. I learned to network, MSW style, by being a good listener. You can too, Ben."

"I don't have to talk to 1,600 people, do I?" Ben asked.

"No," I said, "I just want you to know that you have way more than 16. And I think you need to read Chapter Three as well as Chapter Four."

"Okay, Coach, you got me." He ate the last cookie. "I'll do my reading. Rachel, thank you for your help. I'm glad you're on my team. And you too, sweetie."

It's one of the things I liked about Ben. If he was wrong about something, he'd admit it and make it right.

"And Orville," he said, "That line about Michelangelo toiling alone? If I hadn't had two people mad at me, I would have laughed out loud. Nice try, coach."

Real Networking

An Authentic Conversation
No gimmicks. Be yourself.

Common Interest
There is a basis for the conversation.

Information Exchange
People learn from each other.

| DECIDE | **PREPARE** | TALK | LAND |

Chapter Four

Real Networking and How It Works

I have eaten only vegetarian food—no meat, fish, or fowl—for 30 years. When I first started eating that way, it was unfashionable. In restaurants, I sometimes had to order special dishes that weren't on the menu. I usually didn't tell people I was vegetarian, because it was thought a little strange.

These days, it's not so unusual. In some places, it's even quite fashionable. It's considered healthy. Vegetarian menu items have become much more common. In fact, the last time I checked, even Burger King had a veggie burger.

Sometimes when I'm leading seminars small enough to have a discussion, I talk about vegetarian restaurants with the group. "Do you know of any vegetarian restaurants?" is how I usually start. Most of the time, there is at least one person in the room who can name a vegetarian restaurant, or one with vegetarian items on the menu. Depending on the city, sometimes everyone in the room can name more than one.

My second question is, "Do you know anyone who might know more about vegetarian restaurants than you do?" This usually gets the group talking. Even when no one knows of a vegetarian restaurant, there are usually several people who have friends who eat a vegetarian diet. So we talk about the eating habits of sisters and brothers, aunts and uncles, spouses and friends. People tell stories.

In that conversation, I listen for people who say things like, "My friend Frank has been a vegetarian for many years. He loves to go to restaurants." Then I'll say, "Would you be comfortable introducing me to Frank? I'd be interested in hearing what he says about the local vegetarian restaurants. I'm going to be here only for a week, and I'd like to try some of the better ones."

I watch the person's face to see if they would really be comfortable in making the introduction. If they're not, I let it go and try another person.

By now, most of the people in the room have figured out that this is a networking demonstration. So I stop doing the veggie thing and we talk about networking.

All of us use networking all the time as a way of collecting the practical information we need in order to solve problems and live happier lives. When I teach networking as a job-hunting tool, the first thing I want people to notice is how comfortable and natural networking conversations are.

It looks to me like networking is used all the time in all cultures. We don't usually call it networking. We call it "talking to people." It's how we learn. We all do it as part of normal social conversations. At work, it can happen on breaks, standing around the water cooler or coffeepot. In the rest of life, it happens on the phone or in e-mails and text messages—as well as in person.

Sometimes it's a little more obvious at work. When that new software upgrade comes out, for example, you might call Jeff to ask how to use the gizmo feature. Jeff says he doesn't know, but tells you to call Sally in accounting. So you call her and have a little chat about Jeff and how his favorite baseball team is on a losing streak. Then she tells you how the gizmo works. That's networking.

Real Networking

An authentic conversation.

Common interest.

Information exchange.

I think there are three things that are important about networking. First, it needs to be an authentic conversation. That means nobody's faking it. It's real. It's comfortable. It's not awkward. There are no hidden agendas or attempts to manipulate. It's two people having a chat. Or maybe a more serious conversation. But they're both being who they are.

That might seem totally obvious, but it looks to me like it's the point most commonly missed when job hunters do networking.

Second, there is a shared interest of some kind. When you call Jeff at the office, the two of you share an interest in getting the new software working. You share an even more fundamental common interest, because you are both employed by the same organization.

When you talk to Sally, the gizmo genius, the two of you share the same two interests, the software, and your employer. You and Sally have the additional common interest of Jeff. You both know him. Maybe you both like him. And you're both familiar with his fanatical devotion to his baseball team.

In the other example, the obvious common interest is vegetarianism. When other people share my interest in that topic, that shared interested powers the conversation. But underlying that is the much more powerful common interest: we're all in the same seminar together. And we're all there because we're all interested in job hunting, the topic of the seminar.

The third element of real networking is information exchange. We're talking about a particular topic and sharing information back and forth on that topic. In the vegetarian example, I selected the topic and started the conversation. But anyone could do it.

Sometimes the conversation starts with one common interest and moves from there into other shared interests and other topics. So with Sally, you talked about Jeff and his baseball team before you talked about gizmos.

Here are more examples of real life networking:

NEW MOMS, GOLFERS, AND CAR BUYERS

Imagine that there's a woman who recently had her first child. Now she's walking in the mall with her baby in a stroller, heading for the baby clothes store. Just as she's arriving, another young mother approaches from the other direction with a baby of about the same age, also in a stroller.

The shared interests are so obvious and so powerful that the two of them stop and talk, even though they never met before. The conversation topics are entirely predictable: baby clothes, care, and feeding of infants, childbirth, and pediatricians are all likely possibilities. In the information exchange on any of these topics, both women are likely to pick up some useful facts and ideas.

While these two strangers are talking, they're also deciding whether they like each other. If there's no chemistry between them, the conversation will probably be brief. They'll go their separate ways.

On the other hand, if there is some chemistry and the babies are not demanding attention, the conversation could continue. If they discover further common interests, it will go even longer. The talk could then easily move to related topics such as other children, husbands, or work. If one or both was on maternity leave, there could be a conversation about when—or whether—to return to work. If one was unemployed and feeling the need for higher family income, the conversation could turn to job hunting.

Now imagine that these two women were friends before the babies were born. Everything gets even easier. Before the babies, they were both in the same Friends Network. Now they have both joined a New Mother Network. It's a double dose of common interests. The conversation can and will go anywhere.

Just as new mothers pick up a lot of useful information on the New Mother Network, golfers get the lowdown on golfing equipment, golf courses, pros, and how to improve their swings on the Golfer Network. Prospective car buyers learn about new cars on the Internet and by reading car magazines. But often the information they value most is what they get in the Car Owner Network.

And of course, if you were planning to buy a new car, you'd talk to your golfing buddies, wouldn't you?

So my first point is simple. We all learn all kinds of things every day in comfortable authentic conversations with people who share some of our interests. Plenty of information exchange happens, but it's not usually called networking. And it's certainly not called information interviewing. You don't usually plan it, but you do it intentionally—as in, "tomorrow on the golf course, I've got to ask Frank about his Lexus hybrid."

My second point is the important one. Many job hunters don't do any of this. They break all the rules. They try to have conversations where there is no common interest at all. It's not about information exchange. It's not even about information. They focus on job openings and inappropriately ask for favors. They call it networking. But it's not.

You can't blame them, because there are job-hunting books and networking books that recommend all kinds of things in the name of networking. I've actually seen books that suggest inauthenticity—and even outright lying—as part of job search networking.

What the Networking Experts Say

Theoretically, you can reach anyone on the planet through six degrees of separation.

In reality, job hunters usually succeed at the second and third degree of separation.

You will probably go from a strong connection to one or two weaker ones to a job.

In my early years in job-search assistance, I saw so many of those strange ideas about networking that I went completely outside of the job-hunting field to be sure I understood what real networking is and how it works. The first book I read was *The Networking Book: People Connecting with People*, a 1986 Routledge & Kegan Paul publication by Jessica Lipnack and Jeffrey Stamps. The book had a foreword by Buckminster Fuller, who was then associated with all kinds of cool new ideas.

When Lipnack and Stamps began their research in the late 1970s, there was a great deal of discussion about networks replacing hierarchies. Networking was just becoming popular. The authors produced their book by networking with people who were interested in effective networking. Through their own networking, Lipnack and Stamps compiled a list of 50,000 people and organizations, contacted 4,000 of them, and collected information from 1,500. I have always liked the simple definitions that they gleaned from all their work:

"A network is a web of free-standing participants cohering through shared values and interests."

"Networking is people connecting with people, linking ideas and resources." (page 2)

My favorite recent book on the subject, published in 2003 by W.W. Norton, is *Six Degrees: The Science of a Connected Age*, by Dr. Duncan Watts, a professor at Columbia University. I had the good fortune to meet Professor Watts when he and I were both being filmed for an ABC TV show on networking. So I bought his book.

He's one very smart guy. His PhD is in theoretical and applied mechanics. He has published articles in academic journals in the fields of physics and sociology. His book covers computer networks and biological networks as well as the social networks we're talking about here.

He makes every effort to explain things in plain English, and I can honestly say that I fully understood some parts of it. It's not the first book I would recommend for job hunters, but I picked up some information that's very useful in my work.

What I liked best, of course, were the parts that had a bearing on job hunting. He mentions "network structure" defining it as "the observed set of ties linking the members of a population like a firm, a school, or a political organization." (page 48) He also talks about the subgroups or clusters that exist within networks and are "based on shared experience, location, or interests."(page 40) This "clustering" concept is important in job-search networking, and we'll talk more about it later in this chapter.

I'm telling you all this because I believe that in order to be highly effective in job hunting, you need to understand what real social networking is and operate in ways that the experts have validated and that ordinary people have found to work. I also want you to know that the ideas of information exchange and common interests are not just things I made up. They're derived from the ideas of people who have thought very carefully about networks and how they work— as well as from my own experience with job hunters.

To make sure we cover the basics of real networking, let's use a couple of diagrams. If you've seen this before, please skip on ahead to the section titled "Don't Forget the Clustering," so you can see what Professor Watts said about clusters inside of networks.

First, let's look at the diagram of You and Your Network on page 70. That's you, the white circle in the middle. The 10 black circles are people you are connected with. The lines represent the common interests that connect you with the others. That's a simple network: You and 10 people at the first degree of separation. In fact, you belong to multiple networks, each defined by a different set of common interests. I like to use the phrase "Total Network" for the sum of all of those networks added together.

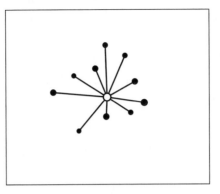

You and Your Network
First Degree of Separation

Some of your networks may be smaller than the 10 people I've shown in the diagram. Most are larger. I hope it's obvious that your Total Network is much, much larger. I used 10 here because it makes the arithmetic easy.

Now, just for a moment, let's assume that your Total Network is only 10 people. And let's also assume that each of those 10 also has a Total Network of 10. That means that you could theoretically reach out through the 10 people you know, and touch a total of 100 people at the first and second degree of separation. That diagram is below.

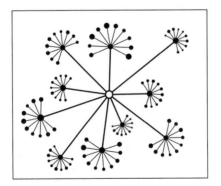

You and Your Network
Two Degrees of Separation

And then, theoretically, each of those hundred also knows 10 people, which would allow you to reach a thousand more people at the third degree of separation. And 10,000 more at the fourth degree of separation—theoretically. I won't do a diagram, because you get the idea already. And we'd need a piece of paper much bigger than the page you're looking at.

Suppose that we wanted to illustrate the entire Six Degrees of Separation, the idea that you can theoretically create a chain of introductions to meet anyone on the planet with a chain of six introductions. There is no piece of paper large enough. Assuming a modest Total Network of 100 per person, you're theoretically reaching 100 million at the fourth degree of separation and a trillion at the sixth degree of separation—more people than there are on the planet.

But all of this is highly theoretical and not so sophisticated. Let's get more practical and a little bit more sophisticated.

DON'T FORGET THE CLUSTERING

This six-degree, pyramiding kind of thing has been widely repeated in books on networking. But it's important to add the part about "clustering" that we learned from Professor Watts. It's not complicated, this one. You may have already noticed it.

Some of the 10 people represented by the black circles in our original diagram know each other as well as knowing you, so they're a cluster. And many of the people they know also know each other. Therefore, you're not reaching 10,000 people at the fourth degree of separation. There's a whole bunch of duplication.

In job hunting, this really doesn't matter, because the numbers are so huge. You know more than 10 people. You don't need anywhere near 10,000 people to succeed. So the numbers work just fine.

What is important in a job search is this: It's sometimes useful to reach out beyond your immediate circle and outside of the networks where you spend most of your time. Although those are useful and should be pursued, sometimes it's exactly the "odd" contact—the person you wouldn't normally talk to—that connects you with a whole new group of people, a completely different cluster.

In this book, I am teaching a systematic method of job-search networking. I do that because most job hunters are anything but systematic, and being systematic in your networking is an important part of being effective in your job search. However, Professor Watts provides us with evidence that it can be very productive to sometimes network with people who seem to have no connection to where you want to go, people who are quite different from those you normally talk to.

SIX DEGREES OF SEPARATION?

There's one more thing that Professor Watts mentioned on page 49 of his book that I want you to know. This actually came from another professor, Mark Granovetter, a sociologist. Professor Watts tells us that Granovetter called it "the strength of weak ties," and it has been widely discussed in job-search assistance circles for many years. What he means by this is that job hunters are more likely to get connected to their next job through someone they know less well rather than through their best friends.

This does not mean that you should ignore your best friends. They're your best starting point. But my own experience in working with job hunters points in the same direction in which Granovetter pointed: you are not so likely to make the final connection to your next employer with your best friends, at the first degree of separation. It's probably a weaker connection.

But on the other hand, it's not about six degrees of separation. The action in job hunting is mostly in the second and third degree of separation.

And there's another way that it's easier, too. You may have noticed by now that in talking about networks, we are also sometimes talking about communities and relationships. Let's take a more careful look at each of those and how they make job-search networking easier.

Networking, Communities, and Relationships

Networking inside a community is easier.
Strong personal relationships accelerate the process.
In both cases, people are predisposed to assist you.

You could say that a community is a network, and it is. But it's also a great deal more than a network.

A simple example is this: imagine that you're a stamp collector. As such, you are a member of the global stamp collecting network. You share that interest with many people. Now imagine that you live in Smallville, and you are the founder of the Smallville Stamp Collectors Club.

The six of you in that club meet every Tuesday evening, and over time your discussions go far beyond stamps. You all live in Smallville, so you share other common interests. You get to know each other. You build relationships. You come to really care about each other. You become a smaller community inside of the Smallville community.

Communities are held together not only by common interests, but also by shared values and personal relationships. The more central those shared values are in the lives of community members, the more powerful the connections between the people. It goes far beyond stamp collecting.

Communities aren't merely about sharing information, they're also about a sense of fellowship, a sense of belonging that is more powerful than a network. In many communities, there is also a strong sense of pulling together, supporting each other, and helping each other.

One interest that community members usually share is a concern for the common good. There may also be a concern for the welfare of individual members of the community. In some communities, that concern is apparent even in situations where two community members have never met each other—where there is no relationship at all.

In addition to having common interests (just as networking partners do), community members share common goals and value systems. The shared concern we just looked at is actually indicative of a value system. Some communities are tightly knit groups in which people stick together and help each other through thick and thin.

Think of a frontier farming community in the early days of the United States, for example. Facing numerous external threats, members of those communities banded together to protect and assist each other. Happily, this same spirit of cooperation still exists today, especially in smaller towns. That's also a value system, one that emphasizes mutual assistance.

Religious organizations—churches and synagogues, for example—are sometimes just as tightly knit, or more so. People stick together and help each other. They share important life events, like births, weddings, and deaths. They have a strongly held shared value system that includes religious beliefs and standards for behavior.

Another example is the family. It can also be seen as a small community. Or a large one, a clan. Again, it's not just community. It's also relationships, usually strong relationships.

In many of these communities, people helping each other is a cultural norm. They don't talk about it. It's not seen as asking for favors or doing favors. It's just the way it is. People help each other.

On the other hand, the bonds between people in some communities are not nearly so strong. A suburban residential community where most residents commute to work in the city might be in this category. It is a community, and there are shared interests and shared activities. However, there might be less of a shared value system—and relationships may not be as strong. But still, people are inclined to help each other.

I have seen groups in business that look to me like communities would. One example is women in management roles, especially higher level management roles. Because they all have to deal with the "glass ceiling" in one way or another, they tend to band together when they can to share experiences and assist each other. Other minority groups sometimes have similar experiences. Any of these groups might also have a formal organization.

Senior executives are another example, especially when the executives are the highest position in an organization—president, CEO, or the equivalent. They literally have no peers in the organization and therefore are sometimes quite interested in getting together with other executives who understand this unique situation and are struggling with similar problems and issues. I think it could be considered a community. It's almost a club.

In job hunting, you may be a member of some networks that are also communities. If so, and if the communities have a strong sense of mutual support, it's much easier to do job-search networking. Even people you don't know well may be more than willing not only to share information, but also to actively assist.

NETWORKING AND RELATIONSHIPS

As we've already noticed, you have strong relationships with some people who are members of your networks and your communities. You know each other well. You trust each other. You care about each other. There's been some real give and take over a long time. You have a shared history as well as shared interests. Talking to these people is usually the easiest way to get your job search going.

But you don't need to have a strong relationship with someone to network—or exchange information—with them. Whenever you're considering networking with someone, I think it's important to ask yourself what the strength of the relationship is. And then act accordingly.

I'm saying all this because job hunters are sometimes advised to ask all of their networking contacts for "20 minutes of your time." If the relationship is strong enough, that works just fine. You could get an hour or more if you wanted to. But doing that kind of thing where there is no relationship involved can simply be making a nuisance of yourself and actually damaging your reputation.

Most of the people in your friend and family networks are people you have strong relationships with, which means you both might be comfortable with your asking them for some concrete assistance that goes beyond networking. This can include reviewing your Target List, mapping their own network to actively look for people you might want to meet, doing an information interview, or locating someone with whom you can do an information interview.

And when you're introduced to a new person by someone you have a strong relationship with, the strength of that relationship will probably carry over and make the new contact easier.

HOW NETWORKING CAN GO WRONG IN JOB HUNTING

In job hunting, people sometimes fail to notice the difference be-tween networking as a member of a community and networking outside of any community—or in a community of which they're not a member.

They confuse their network contacts with relationships or community connections. When that happens, the job hunter may initiate an inappropriate conversation, one that makes both parties un-comfortable. Those conversations, of course, are not very productive.

Networking, as we have noted, is information exchanged between people who share a common interest. With most people who are in this category—and *only* in this category—it's not appropriate to go beyond information exchange.

In other words, it's only about a conversation, not about their *doing* anything to help you (unless maybe there's some benefit for them in it). It's certainly not about them going out of their way to assist you in your search. Some may choose to do that, but it's not a reasonable expectation if the connection is *only* a network connection.

But when the network contact is also a community contact or someone with whom you have a strong relationship, it's completely different.

For example, I have sometimes seen job hunters do most or all of their networking inside of a single community, such as a church or synagogue. That could be a single synagogue in one town, or it could be working with churches of the same denomination in two or more cities. The latter is sometimes an excellent way to do job hunting when you're moving to a new town.

REAL NETWORKING IN THE JOB SEARCH

I've taken the time to talk about the definition of real networking, because the most successful job hunters do their job-search networking in exactly the same way that they always do networking. It's all about authentic conversations where everyone is comfortable. It's about shared interests. The focus is on information.

These authentic networkers find jobs and enhance their reputations while doing it. And because they understand how networking really works, they're also successful in helping others find jobs—as well as resources and information on practically any topic.

When people have problems with job-search networking, it's often because they ignore these basic principles. They behave in inauthentic ways, sometimes even in ways that are not consistent with their own values. They ask for big favors in situations where asking for favors isn't appropriate. And their conversations are all about job openings or "who's hiring," topics that virtually nobody has information on—and topics that make many people uncomfortable.

So it looks to me like one key issue in job-search networking is using the real definition of networking and staying with the way that networking is normally done. This means having friendly conversations with people you have some kind of connection with, some kind of common interest, weak or strong. And if you also have a strong relationship or a community connection, it's even easier.

This is completely different from cold calling, where you are trying to get a total stranger to talk to you. One is more like calling your cousin. Or a friend of your cousin's. The other is more like selling aluminum siding to a stranger.

Now that we've looked at what real networking is and is not, I hope you have a definition that will be a solid foundation for an effective job search. And I hope that by now you've decided to incorporate highly effective networking into your search.

In the next chapter, we will map out your networks so you can see their extent and which of them will be the most useful and easiest to use.

ORVILLE'S JOURNAL

Engineers, Managers, and Alicia the Sociologist

"Orville, my total network reach is in the quintillions. If I start with 1,600 people, and each of them has 1,600, it's 10 to the 19th (10^{19}) people. More or less." We were back in the Williams' living room again, and our discussion was moving to Chapter Four.

Ben had single-handedly eaten all of the cookies, just like last time. Only this time, Jessie had put out a smaller tray. And this time, Ben was eating more slowly. Now he poured a cup of coffee.

Rachel looked at Jessie. "He's kind of geeky, isn't he?"

"Yes," she said, "Isn't it cute?"

"Cute wasn't the first word that came to mind. But at least he sees that his network is bigger than 16 people."

"Having a huge network isn't the point," I put in, hoping Ben hadn't missed that part. First he was way low. Now he had read two more chapters and was wildly overshooting.

"I know," he said. "The point is that Rachel knows some people in the engineering department. And my beloved wife is going to set me up with 11 people. I'm off and running."

Ah, I thought, he was just playing with us. "Ben," I said, "You ate all the cookies again. There were 10 squared (10^2) cookies and now there are zero."

"And Orville," Jessie added, "You didn't eat any. You used to be the local Cookie Monster. What happened?"

"I discovered fruit," I said. "I switched to pears, apples, and grapes. On special occasions, I might even eat a little pineapple. And no coffee. Jasmine tea."

"There's a prof at The Wall like that," Rachel said. "You should meet her."

"What's The Wall?" Ben asked.

I'd probably like her," I replied, "Common interests. Is she veggie? What's she do?"

"Walcott. We call it The Wall. Yes, veggie. A sociologist."

"Rachel," I said, "You're really good at this networking stuff. You never stop."

"Maybe she knows that other sociologist you mentioned, Orville, the weak connections guy." Ben was half finished with his coffee.

"You could ask her. Her name's Alicia." Rachel said.

"I'd like to meet her," I said.

"I liked the part about the second and third degree of separation," Jessie said. "It makes sense. It's not about friends, it's the friends of friends."

"I agree," Rachel put in. "That's how it usually works. Sometimes you know who knows. But usually you have to figure out which of your friends might know who knows."

Ben smiled. "It's like a big puzzle. I think I can actually do this," he said. "With a little help from my friends, of course."

"Watch out," Rachel said, "Ben's going to be a social butterfly."

"I don't think you have to worry about that. But I could talk to people more. I was just thinking about communities and networks."

"Sometimes you think the only community you belong to is the engineering community," Jesse offered. "But there's lots of others."

Yes," he agreed. "The church community is also a huge network. I volunteered in the job search assistance program for a while. Now I'm going to go over and join the Job Search Work Team. And we're a little community right here." He paused for a minute, thinking.

"My engineering community is a group I've worked with for years. Guys I know in other companies and see sometimes. But I'm in an engineering network too. It's a global engineering network. We talk all the time by e-mail."

"Ben," I said, "I think you just wrote Chapter Five. It's all about mapping your various networks. And if they're communities too, so much the better."

"Before you guys write Chapter Five, can we finish talking about Chapter Four?" Rachel was just finishing her first and only cup of herbal tea. "We haven't talked about the most important part."

"What's that?" Ben asked. "Authenticity?"

"No," she said. "You're already authentic. I don't think you could change that part. It's clustering."

"Why do I care about clustering when I have quintillions of possible networking contacts?"

"Because you're not going to talk to quintillions of people. You're going to talk to engineers, engineering managers, and manufacturing people. And that's good. It's the right cluster. But you don't want to be stuck in that cluster for your whole job search. You should meet Alicia too."

"Alicia? She won't know the right people. She's a sociologist. Why her?"

"You don't know who she knows. And that's the point. I actually think the two of you would enjoy each other."

"But what's the common interest?"

"Me, I suppose. And she thinks like you do. Very analytical. You both make the same kind of geeky comments sometimes. You should meet her. I think you'd like each other."

"Jessie," I said, "You're right. Rachel is a networking genius."

"Let's see if they actually meet and get along before we leap to that conclusion," Rachel said. "But we've now discussed all of Chapter Four."

Your Total Network Is:

The sum of all the networks that you belong to.

All of your active, dormant, and passive contacts.

Anyone who would readily take your phone call.

| DECIDE | **PREPARE** | TALK | LAND |

Chapter Five

Your Total Network Is Bigger Than You Think

For more than 30 years now, I've had a lot of conversations with a lot of different people about networking. One question that I have often asked is, "How big is your Total Network?"

I'll ask you that question right now. How many people are there in your Total Network? When you add together all the people in all of the networks of which you're a member, how many people is that? Ten? A hundred? A thousand? Ten thousand? Fifty thousand?

How many?

When I initially ask that question in a networking seminar, people usually estimate the size of their networks between a half dozen and a couple hundred people. I know from experience that those initial numbers are far too small. Even a monk living in a monastery has a Total Network larger than 200.

Sometimes I'll rephrase the question and try again: "I'm not just talking about the people you might be willing to have a job hunting conversation with. I'm talking about all of the people you have a network connection with, whether you would contact them in your job search or not."

Occasionally, that expanded question gets people to enlarge their estimates, but they don't get much larger. By the end of the seminar, however, the numbers usually range between a thousand and tens of thousands. The vast majority of people initially underestimate the size of their Total Network by quite a lot.

If you are one of those rare people who already knows that your Total Network includes thousands of people, you may not need to do the exercises in this chapter. But please don't skip the chapter entirely, because we'll also be laying some additional groundwork for effective networking.

On the other hand, if you're thinking that you're the exception to the rule, the one person who really does have a very limited network, welcome to the club. It's a big club, the people who initially believe that. If you're in that club, please keep reading. You may even need to read this chapter twice. And please do *all* of the exercises.

Unless you've literally lived by yourself in a cave for your entire life—with the same person bringing your food every day—your network is more than adequate. The question isn't really the size of your network. The question is whether you're willing to take a good hard look at all aspects of your personal network. And the big question—the important one if you're in a job search—is whether you're willing to make the effort to understand and effectively use that network to find a great new job.

It's not uncommon for a job search to stall out because the job hunter believes that they have "run out of contacts." I want to make sure that does not happen to you. That's why I'm pressing the issue and that's why I want you to spend some time mapping all of the networks that make up your Total Network. You might recall that mapping your networks is the first step in "Prepare for Job Hunting" in the Decide-Prepare-Talk-Land sequence we discussed in Chapter Two.

In mapping your networks, I am going to ask you to consider absolutely everyone you have a network connection with. Not just those you would include in your job-search networking, not just those you talk to regularly, not just those you really want to talk to right now—all of them.

The reason I do it this way is simple: By examining your entire network and thinking about all possible connections without censoring any of them, you may discover useful connections that you didn't know—or forgot—you had.

I am going to ask you to list a large number of network connections, but I am not suggesting that you contact all of them. The list will be a resource list, and a way of seeing where your resources might be. It will be something you later come back to—a place you go to select names of people you want to talk to.

The first step in this process is to define what we mean by your Total Network. Let's start by looking at your job search as a whole and all the ways you can make contact.

Three Ways to Make Contact

1. Talk to people in your networks, people you already have a connection with.

2. Talk to people you are introduced to by current connections.

3. Talk to total strangers. (This is cold calling, not networking.)

To conduct an effective search, you need to talk to a lot of people. There are three ways that you can do this. First, you can talk to people you already have some kind of connection with, some common interest. In other words, you can use the network you already have.

Second, you can talk to people that you have been introduced to by someone you have some kind of connection with. This process of getting introductions is what is usually called "networking," and we'll talk more about it in Chapters Seven and Eight. These new people that you'll be introduced to are not part of your current network, though they may join it. You may need to meet a lot of new people or just a few.

Or, third, you can talk to total strangers, people who have never heard of you, people to whom you have not been introduced. This is not networking at all. It's cold calling, the stuff telemarketers or door-to-door salespeople do. For most salaried job hunters in most situations, this is a difficult, uncomfortable, and marginally effective technique.

The big dividing line in job hunting, then, is between situations in which you have a connection or introduction and those in which you don't. The former are sometimes called "warm" contacts and the latter "cold contacts."

If you use cold contacts, what you're doing is what salespeople call "cold calling"—not networking. Warm contacts will accept a phone call from you, sometimes with a little hesitation, and sometimes gladly and with great delight. Your current network, new people your current network introduces you to and people those new people introduce you to—are all warm contacts. Obviously, some are warmer than others. But none are cold.

Based on all of that, I believe this is the most useful definition for the purpose of mapping your current Total Network and using it in job search:

Your Total Network Is Everyone Who Will Accept a Phone Call From You

Your Total Network is composed of all the people who will accept a phone call from you right now, without an introduction from a mutual acquaintance. Some of these are people you know well, people who will recognize your name immediately so the conversation is off to a fast start. With the rest of your Total Network, you will need to remind them of how you are connected or point out a connection of which they may not be aware. Here are some examples:

I'm Pat Person from Lee Hecht Harrison. (Or from the church, the Home & School Association, or from down the street—whatever will help them place you).

This is Pat Person. I don't know if you remember, but we met at the Prescott University Management Seminar in Chicago last December.

This is Pat Person calling. We haven't talked for years, but we were classmates at Prescott University. You might remember me from French class. I usually sat in the third row, right behind you.

This is Pat Person. I don't believe we've ever met, but we're both graduates of Pennsbury High School in Yardley, Pennsylvania. I believe I was several years ahead of you, a senior when you were a sophomore.

My name is Pat Person. You may not remember me, but we both worked at United Amalgamated in Houston in the late 1990's. At that time, I believe you were in Domestic Operations. I was in HR.

Some of these connections are strong. Some are weak. But all are enough to get a conversation started. If the conversation produces other areas of shared interest, it will generate a stronger connection.

I'm not saying that you will have to do a lot of these "reminder" introductions of yourself. It's too soon to know if you'll need to or not. Right now, we're mapping your Total Network, so you can see where all the possible contacts are. After we've done that, you'll prioritize the contacts and see which ones you'll use—and which ones you won't.

Three Kinds of Network Connections:

Active—contacts you talk to regularly.

Dormant—contacts you used to talk to regularly.

Passive—network connections that have not been activated.

Your Total Network includes active connections with people you talk to once a year or more. Friends, coworkers, and fellow members of any organization are all examples of active connections. If you had a connection with someone that was once an active connection, but you haven't talked to them for a year or more, that connection can be called a dormant connection.

You can reactivate dormant connections by getting back in touch and catching up on what's happened in the intervening years. Sometimes that's a really great thing to do, whether you're in a job search or not. In other cases, it might be better to let sleeping dogs lie.

There are also passive connections, those that have never been active, but are based on a common interest and could be activated. (That's the previous "same high school" example.) These are often organizational connections.

Any graduate of West Point, for example, has a network connection to any other graduate, whether they have met or not. In fact, this is a triple connection, because all are connected with the U.S. Army, all are officers, and all are alumni of the same college. Any two West Pointers who talk to each other will probably find additional experiences in common beyond those three.

If you decide to reach out to members of your Total Network where the connection is a passive one, you're taking a risk. They may not see the connection as strong enough to warrant talking to you. There may be little or no chemistry between the two of you.

On the other hand, sometimes the conversation takes off. The two of you really enjoy getting acquainted and both want to stay in touch. You'll need to decide if and when you want to take the risk of making calls to passive network connections. They usually work best when there is more than one passive connection, as in the case of the West Point graduate.

Please estimate the size of your Total Network right now. Has the number gone up from your initial estimate, the one you made at the beginning of this chapter? Whether it has or not, I'm going to keep working with you on increasing it.

Before you finish this chapter, you'll list the names of all the networks that make up your Total Network. You'll actually write them on paper or type them on your computer and then list some actual names of people that are fellow members of each of those sub-networks. But before you make the list, let's zoom out a bit and take a broader look at what we're doing here.

Mapping Your Networks

Make a list of networks you belong to.

List names of people associated with each.

Note passive network connections for each.

Your Total Network is made up of numerous smaller networks. These smaller networks sometimes overlap, so that some people you know belong to several of your networks. These overlaps can be a nuisance when you're making lists, but noticing them is very useful. Someone who belongs to a number of your networks is someone who shares a number of common interests with you, just like those West Point Army officers. That person might be a very useful connection in a job search.

The first step in mapping your networks is making a list of the various networks to which you belong. Remember, each of these networks is defined by some common interest. There is a list of the names of some common networks on page 90 This is a good starting point, but it's important that you include all of your networks, whether they are on my list or not. And please use your own name for your networks, whatever name is convenient and meaningful for you.

If you're in a job search right now or planning to start one soon, please pick up a pen and begin listing your own networks as you read. If you think of names of people who belong to each network, note those along with the name of the network.

Mapping Your Networks
A sample of common networks

Educational networks
College or university
High school, grade school
Specialized education or training

Employment networks
Your current employer
Past employers
Vendors, customers, and clients of each
Strategic partners of each

Other organizational networks
Religious/spiritual
Fraternal/Sororal
Alumni
Professional
Political
Community
Service, charitable

Personal business networks
Banker, broker, lawyer
Doctor, dentist
Accountant, financial advisor

Avocational networks
Golf, tennis, basketball, sports
Hobbies

Other networks
Family
Friends
Community
Neighbors, past and present

Here's why I'm asking you to do this: People who believe that their network is very small have difficulties in job search—unnecessary difficulties. I'm an instructional designer as well as a job-search expert, and it looks to me like actually writing things down is an enormous help in this particular part of the process. So I'm inviting you to try it. Write while you're reading.

I'd like to suggest that you do not go to any of your address books, phone books, directories, Websites, PDAs, or databases. Not yet. Think first. See if you can come up with people that maybe aren't included in any of those sources. Then go to the other sources to expand the list.

Anyway, I'm going to comment on some of the more common networks to make sure that I'm clearly communicating what I mean by the list on page 90. My intention, of course, is to stimulate your thinking about your own networks. Please write down names of your networks and names of associated people as you read. If you own this book, it's okay with me if you write in the margins.

Your College Network

I'm starting here because it's a simple starting point. Although it may or may not be your best network, it's one people often think of. If you went to college, you met people there. You took courses, maybe 32, maybe 40, maybe more. In each of those courses you sat in a classroom with a lot of other people, maybe a dozen or maybe a hundred or more. You lived in dorms or apartments, maybe with roommates, and you met people socially, in sports and in other activities.

If you're a recent graduate, you may have a lot of active network connections from college. If you graduated 40 years ago, maybe most of them are now dormant, but they're still network connections and you can reactivate some of them if you want to.

Finally, you can and should consider every living human being who ever attended that college a passive member of your college alumni network. Theoretically, you could activate your connection with any of them, whether you ever met them or not. In the real world, your connections with members of your own graduating class are likely to be the strongest, and those passive connections are likely to be the easiest to activate.

But please notice that your graduating class is the easiest because it's actually a triple common interest: same school, same year (so you probably had some shared experiences there), and probably the same age. You probably have multiple shared interests with members of other classes, too. The same major, the same sport or activity, the same sorority/fraternity, or the same home state are all examples.

I was recently on the receiving end of a networking call like this. I got a call from a woman who had graduated from Yale University, my alma mater, many years after I had graduated. We had never met, but she was pleasant and very well informed. She had obviously done her homework. I was initially wary, wondering if she was going to ask for a donation for something. But she quickly got to the point.

She told me that she had several years experience with a business consulting firm and was now exploring moving to consulting in the Human Resources area. She knew that I worked for Lee Hecht Harrison and she knew that LHH did HR consulting. So we had three shared interests: Yale, LHH, and HR consulting. We had a pleasant conversation about all three. She got some useful information. And I learned a couple of things too.

In considering college networks, please remember that we're not talking about contacting everyone who ever went to good old State U. We're just talking about recognizing that huge network and your membership in it. And we're talking about carefully surveying that network to see what your resources are. Later, you may decide to use some of them in job hunting. And, like the Yalie, you may decide to seek out alums you've never met, but who share other interests with you.

There is also an organizational network related to your college or university, the alumni organization. Many schools have alumni clubs that meet regularly. Belonging to one can be useful in career management, as well as in job search. Your college alumni office or career development center may be able to help you make alumni connections. They may even have a database you can search. It's worth looking into.

Employer Networks

If you have had work experience of any kind, anywhere, you are a member of one or more of employer networks. You should consider each of your past employers as a separate organizational network. These employer networks are particularly useful in job hunting—which is why I included them as a separate category on page 90 even though they are also organizational networks.

At each of your former employers, there are a number of people who not only know you but—even more important—know you at work. If your reputation was average or better, the majority of those people will speak well of you and may be willing to assist you in taking your next career step. If the organization was a large one, there might be dozens or even hundreds of people who know you by reputation, as well as those who had direct experience working with you.

In addition, all current and former employees of organizations where you have worked can be considered passive network contacts in the same way that all graduates of your college can. Again, I am certainly not suggesting that you will contact all of them. But I want to make sure you are aware of the possibilities and consider them.

Some larger work organizations actually have "alumni" organizations set up by former employees. These organizations do many of the same things that college alumni groups do. You may be able to find them on the Internet or by talking to current employees. If there is no such group, you can find alumni by finding one or two people who worked there when you did and are still there. Friendly reminiscences about what happened to Frank and where did Susan go are usually comfortable and pleasant conversations.

If you are a recent college graduate and your work experience has been limited to nonprofessional summer jobs and not related to the career you want, your employment networks are nonetheless valuable. Don't be concerned that they are not work in your chosen field. These are former employers. They know you as an employee. They can be very useful.

If you are a manager or executive, your job search and networking will, of course, be most effective with managers and executives at former employers. But don't neglect employees below your former level. You want them to be aware of your search, and you don't know who they might know.

You should also consider your external contacts in each of your prior employers. Did you deal with vendors? Banks and other financial organizations? Strategic partners? Managers and executives in other business units? Customers and clients? Any of these can be great networking contacts. Some of them may have a personal stake in your successful employment in the right new job.

Anyone in job search should consider networking at all of their former employers. From time to time, this results in an offer to return to a former company. I have heard of people calling a former boss and getting invited to return on the spot. But that's not the point. The point is that there is a wealth of potential contacts in this category.

If you are currently employed, you need to be cautious about networking inside your current organization for employment outside of it. If you widely advertise your intention to leave, you could be seen as a malcontent and you could create career problems for yourself.

Organizational Networks

Any organization you are a current or past member of is also a network. As we discussed, employers are organizational networks, as are colleges and universities. Professional associations are also organizational networks and well worth belonging to. You are automatically a member of a professional network including all members of your current profession whether you belong to the professional association or not. But belonging to the association can produce additional networking benefits, just as belonging to the alumni club can.

Another organizational network that can be particularly useful in job hunting is a church or synagogue network. As I mentioned, I have seen job hunters whose entire job search has been conducted by networking with members of their church, synagogue, or place of worship.

If you are a member of a religious or spiritual organization, I strongly urge you to network with members of that organization. The more active you have been, the more likely it is to be effective. But even if you recently joined or infrequently attend services, it is well worth doing. Be sure to talk to the leaders in the organization, because they often know the personal and work backgrounds of members and can help you find the right people.

Moreover, many local churches and synagogues are part of a national or even global (think Roman Catholic Church, for example) organization that provides you with links to networks in other cities if you're planning an out of town search. And finally, as we've mentioned, some religious organizations have job-search assistance programs.

In mapping your Total Network, consider all organizations, formal and informal, to which you have ever belonged. This includes political, community, charitable, fraternal/sororal, veterans, clubs, and any other formal or informal organizations.

Personal Business Networks

This is not a major category, but it's always worth considering. Here we are talking about all of those people with whom you do business in your personal life—those people who consider you a client or customer. This might include bankers, brokers, doctors, lawyers, chiropractors, and even massage therapists and hair stylists. All of these people have a personal interest in seeing your employment continued, so that you have a good income to continue doing business with them.

But more importantly, they are all in contact with a large number of people. Some of their clients and customers might very well be the Decision Makers you're looking for. You should certainly make all of them aware of your job search, telling them what kind of work you're looking for, a little bit about the employers you're interested in, and your core message about yourself and your abilities.

Sometimes people think that networking in this category is a bit far-fetched. But I've seen it work repeatedly. The most dramatic example was a job hunter I worked with in a small town in upstate New York. She was a participant in a two-day seminar with me. We discussed networking on the first day and at the end of that day, she left a little bit early to go to a dental appointment.

She decided to try some of the networking things we had been talking about, so she told the dental assistant that she was planning to move to Kansas City and return to her former career of high school teaching.

"Kansas City!" The dental assistant exclaimed. "That's where I'm from! My sister is a high school teacher there! You've got to meet her!"

I can definitely promise you that this does not happen every time. But the point is that you just don't know if it will. Network with people in this category and see what happens. Put them on your list.

Avocational Networks

Networks, as you certainly know by now, are all about shared interests. Therefore, any avocational interest you have makes you a part of a network related to that interest. This might include sports, arts and crafts, gardening, flower arranging, cooking—anything at all. There are people you talk to about that interest. This is the information exchange that's an essential part of networking.

Your networking contacts in this category might all be members of some of your other networks. But it's worth taking a look in this category to see if there are some people here who don't show up elsewhere.

Family and Friends

I saved the two most important categories for last. For just about everyone in job search, family and friends are the two most important networks, and they are also the best place to begin job-search networking. At higher levels of compensation, friends are usually more important. At lower compensation and age levels, it might be family.

There are people in this world who care about you. And you care about them. Some are relatives, some are not. I hope that they are all people you are able to talk to comfortably about a wide range of subjects. Because I want networking to be as easy and comfortable as possible, I usually suggest starting with this group.

People sometimes say, "But none of my friends and relatives are important people. They don't know the right people. They don't travel in the right circles."

That reaction, of course, is based on the myth that networking is about talking to "important" people. If networking is about gathering information and getting a message out on the grapevine, then talking to anyone works. In fact, you don't know exactly who your friends and relatives know until you carefully check into it. The best way to do that is to start networking with them by discussing your job search Project Plan and Target List.

As you may recall from Chapter Four, you are most likely to connect with the Decision Makers in your targeted organizations at the second and third degree of separation. In other words, the most important people in actually connecting you to your next job are probably those you'll be introduced to by people you know now. A strong connection at the first degree of separation—like you have with family and friends—is a great start.

The first question with your friends and relatives is how effective you can be in helping them help you. You will probably need to educate them on job hunting and how job-search networking works. (That could be doing them a favor, right?) And you will certainly want to use your Target List with them, once they understand that it's not about job openings, it's about organizations, information, and people.

We're talking here about a group of people who, like you, and are interested in your success; maybe they're even committed to your success. If you have a Total Network of a thousand or more (and you do, right?), then each of them does too. Although there is certainly some overlap in their networks and yours, there are also large areas where their networks are different from yours. They and you, together, can scan through an enormous number of people, select the best ones to reach out to, and expand your search significantly. These are people you will probably want to talk to repeatedly through the course of your search.

I have ceased to be amazed by the large number of people in job search who fail to do this kind of thing, usually for reasons that make no sense at all: "I don't want to ask for help," for example, or "I don't want to bother them."

If this is you, don't forget to look at it from the other person's point of view. If you were a friend of mine and had something important happening—like a job search, maybe—and you didn't include me, I'd wonder if we were really friends. If I heard from others about it, rather than from you, I might actually be offended.

Now, once again, it's also true that you need to help your friends help. They probably don't know much about a highly effective job search. Most people don't. Everyone thinks of "job openings" or "who's hiring." Then they feel helpless and unable to assist you because they don't know much in either of those categories. When they're uncomfortable, the discussion becomes awkward.

Don't let that happen. Make them comfortable. Help them help you.

While we're on the topic of networking with family, I have an additional message for recent grads, looking for their first "real" jobs, or people in early career generally, in the first 10 years or so. If you're not in that category, please skip on down to the next headline and let me talk to this younger group for a minute.

Family Networking for Recent Grads

Talk to your parents and their friends.
Talk to your friends and their parents.

The most productive things that young, entry-level job hunters can do is to talk to their parents and their parents' friends, and talk to their friends and their friends' parents. In case you haven't noticed yet, I will tell you that parents are pretty much always committed to their adult children's success—highly committed. I'm a parent of adult children myself, as are many of my friends, so I can speak from experience.

They may not always express it well. They might even express it in totally idiotic ways, like trying to talk you into becoming a medical doctor or a salesperson or a teacher because they always wanted to be one. Or trying to talk you out of becoming one of those. Or be generally wanting you to be what they'd hoped to be, or *not* be what they always tried to avoid. Or wanting you to do "better" than they did in some way.

If you can get past this kind of thing and have an adult conversation, parents can be very helpful. This, of course, depends on you being mature enough to handle it. You absolutely need to make your own career decisions, because you'll have to live with them for years. You also have to make your own job search decisions, because you're in charge of this project.

But there's a huge potential advantage here. Your parents are in the same age bracket as many of the Decision Makers to whom you want to talk. If they're also at or above the employment level of those Decision Makers, there's an even bigger advantage. In addition, their network may be bigger than yours simply because they're older. If you can set up an alliance with them for job hunting you'll certainly have an advantage.

Some entry level job hunters balk at allowing their parents to help, especially if their parents are well-placed. The adult child sometimes feels like, "I want to do it myself. I'm an adult now." If this is you, think about it: That may be something left over from adolescence, proving that you're independent of your parents. When you're really independent, you don't have to prove it.

Again, your parents will need to recognize that you're in charge of this project and you make the decisions. They cannot do it for you. You have to interview. You will have to prove yourself on the job. If they can help open some doors, you are the one who needs to walk through those doors, do the right things, tell people what you can do, and be good enough to get and keep the job.

If your parents are unusually powerful and can get someone to hire you sight unseen as a favor to them, please don't allow that to happen. Ask them to help in another way. You need to get the right job for you. That means checking the whole thing out for yourself, not just letting them do it. See if you can find a productive way of working with your powerful parents to meet the people *you* want to meet and take your career in the direction *you* want to go. Talk with them.

On the other hand, suppose that your parents are not well placed. Maybe they're not well educated and work in low-paying jobs. If that's you, please don't make the mistake of writing them off. You don't know who they know unless you include them and talk to them about exactly what you're doing.

So working with your parents and getting introductions to their friends is a great way to go. The other one is just as good: work with your friends and their parents. Sometimes your friends' parents will almost adopt you as their own. Show them the differences between your job search plans and their son's or daughter's so they won't worry about competition.

You and your friend might even talk to them together in a joint planning session. You can get some of the same advantages as with your own parents—and possibly with less friction because neither side has the parent-child baggage to deal with.

Once again, don't assume that they know all about effective job search. They probably don't. I have experience with that generation in job search, and they're no more effective than anyone else. So it might be good to explain what you're doing and why you're doing it that way.

Networking With Your Adult Children

I just talked to younger job hunters. This part is for job hunters with adult children. Here's my message: you can network with them. You should network with them. I mean, hey, what's a family for?

If you're unemployed and embarrassed about it, right now might be a good time to get over that. Your children are adults. They have lives and networks of their own. You don't know exactly what or who they know until you ask. Even if you're a senior executive, they may have information sources useful to you. And approaches you haven't thought of. They have your genes, right? So they're smart.

Why not include them in the project?

Using Your Networks Systematically

Map other people's networks, not just yours.

Make a list to supplement your address book and speed dial.

Treat personal and professional contacts differently.

If you're lucky enough to have friends and relatives willing to put in some real time and effort helping with your job hunting, teach them this approach or ask them to read parts of this book. Then ask them to map their own networks so that the two of you together can figure out where the most promising contacts are and how to get through to them.

One part of friend and family networking that I want to make sure you don't miss is your spouse or partner, if you have one. People sometimes assume that their spouse's network is the same as theirs. Although there is usually a very significant overlap, these two networks are never the same. So don't forget to ask your spouse to map his or her network, and do the same thing you do with other close contacts: discuss it together and create a plan for meeting people.

If you make sure they always have your latest Target List, your spouse, friends, and relatives can network for information on your behalf. They will need to explain to everyone they talk to that it's about information, not job openings. And they should always be on the lookout for people that you can and should meet, especially insiders at your targeted organizations.

MAKE A LIST OF NAMES OF PEOPLE

Okay, now we've gotten to the part that we touched on before we went over the list of networks—the part about listing names of people. If you haven't already done so, please list all of the networks that are part of your Total Network. When you're pretty sure you've got all of them, write the network names as headings, leaving a quarter to half a page of blank paper after each so you can write names of people associated with each network.

You can do this on a computer or write by hand, whichever way you like best. If you're the kind of person who uses a computer a lot, you'll probably want them there sooner or later, in a spreadsheet, database, Word list, or however you like to work. If you prefer to do this kind of thing handwritten—in a three-ring binder, maybe—that's good too.

Now brainstorm the names of people. The idea is to write down every doggone person you can think of. Never mind whether you'd ever want to talk to them about your job search. Never mind whether you'd ever want to talk to them at all. Just write them all down. You'll evaluate them later. If you evaluate and censor now, you'll probably slow the process and end up with fewer possibilities.

Once again, if you have lists of people in an address book, PDA, cell phone, or database, leave those until last. What you're doing here is expanding your list. We are very interested in the people you talk to all the time, but we're also interested in the people you do not talk to regularly, but could if you wanted to.

Sometimes it's exactly that "odd" contact, the person who apparently has nothing to do with what you're looking for, who will connect you to the key Decision Maker. So first work with a blank page, then come back and use your address books, databases, and social networking Websites to round it out.

The bigger your initial resource list of names, the easier it gets to find the right person for the right question—and the right person for the right moment—as your job search unfolds. How big should the total list be? I'd like to see you start with a list of 100. More than that would be even better.

I want you to be clear that there are many, many people you could reach out to. This is true even if you're a 20-something who has always worked alone in the back cubicle—or never worked at all. There's no need to put all of them on paper. I just want you to have the confidence that comes from knowing that they are there if you need them.

PERSONAL AND PROFESSIONAL NETWORKS

We've been talking about labeling all your sub-networks as way to clarify and map your current Total Network, all those people you could talk to if you wanted to. Another useful way to look at your network connections is to distinguish personal and professional network connections.

Your connection to some people is personal. The friends and relatives category is an example of that. You'll probably start your job-search networking with this group because it's easy and comfortable to talk to them and they may be committed to assisting you.

You probably also have a professional network, a group of people you are connected to because you have worked with them. If you have many years of experience, or if you're an executive, or if you're in a field that requires making many contacts, your list of professional contacts might be extensive.

Some of these connections are active. Some are dormant and could be activated. Some are passive, but strong enough that they'd be real possibilities.

These professional contacts are particularly useful in a search because they are knowledgeable about the work you do. They may have seen you in action. They may admire the way you do your job and may be willing to speak very positively of you to others. They are also—all in all—more likely than your personal contacts to know the people you want to meet in your job search.

If you are lucky enough to have some people who are both personal and professional connections, that can be a real advantage. When someone you know and trust is also knowledgeable and connected to the right people, that person might be an excellent person to have an early discussion with—and to work with throughout your search.

As we discussed in the last chapter, everyone has network connections inside of communities they belong to. And everyone has good relationships with at least a few people—and maybe quite a few.

In mapping your networks, think about those places where your networks are inside of communities and where you also have strong relationships. Both of these are great places to get started.

One last point before we wrap up this chapter:

MAP THE NETWORKS OF THE DECISION MAKER

We've been talking about mapping your networks and the networks of people you're connected with so you can see where your resources are. Once you have a Project Plan for your search, there's another useful step you can take. You can map the network of the Decision Makers you want to reach. Although this approach is useful for anyone, it can be particularly useful for managerial and executive level job hunters.

You have a sense of who the Decision Makers are. You know their job titles. You know what organizations they're a part of and you can discover their past organizational connections. You know their approximate compensation level. You might even have a pretty good guess about where they live. Social networking Websites may yield even more information, as will just plain Googling them.

Using this information, you can identify some of the networks they are members of. In other words, you may be able to map at least parts of their Total Network. When you do this, you may find that you are already a member of some of their networks. Or that you have access to some of their networks through some of your network contacts.

For example, you might find that they once worked in the same organization as you did. Or that you have a friend that belongs to the same club they do. You might even find that they graduated from the same college as you. Or that they have children in the same school that your children are in. Even seemingly trivial network connections can turn out to be very useful—as conversation starters if nothing else.

Now that you've mapped your networks—and maybe even some of your Decision Makers' networks—it's time to talk about using networking in creating and implementing your job-hunting project plan. The next chapter is about putting your networks to work in a professional and effective job search.

ORVILLE'S JOURNAL

Ben Decides to Talk to Dormant Contacts, but Not the Guy Who Won the Bet.

"Orville," Rachel said, "I really like your concept of active, dormant, and passive contacts." The four of us were having lunch in the faculty dining room at Walcott. "It's a very useful way to think about network contacts."

"I'm glad you like it." I was picking the slices of fresh pear out of my salad and eating them.

"Remember your myth guy, the one with 5,000 cards on his table," she continued. "Those weren't active contacts. If he talked to each one only once a year, that would be 100 conversations a week. That's possible, I suppose, but I'm not sure why he would do it."

"How many active contacts do you have?" I asked. I was picking out the walnuts and eating them. Pears and walnuts. It was a great salad.

"I call my contacts A's, B's, and C's," she said. "I have about 500 A's, people I talk to at least twice a year. I have about 2,000 B's. I talk to them once every year or two. My C's are what you call dormant and passive. I should really keep better track of them."

"I have 132 active contacts." Ben said. "That's just personal contacts, not counting professional unless they're also personal. Is that enough?"

"Sure," I replied, looking for walnut crumbs, "How many dormant and passive?"

"Hundreds of dormant. Thousands of passive. So you were right, coach, it's much more than 1,600, total. But I'll never call the dormants or passives."

"Why not?" Jessie chimed in. "You have a whole bunch of dormant contacts you should talk to. People you've ignored for years. Like Milton Freid, your Aunt Leslie, and Miles Washington, for example."

"Miles Washington? I'm never going to talk to him. Why would I waste my time calling Aunt Leslie? I've got a job search to do."

"You had a fight with Miles three years ago about a Super Bowl bet. It was $20. You like him. And he's in manufacturing. Why don't you get over it? Pick up the phone."

"Jess is right," I put in. There was nothing left but exotic lettuce. "You should include some dormant contacts. I don't know about those particular people, but I think you should make a list and try a few. Some of them might be even more useful than your actives."

"I agree." Rachel nodded. "Take a closer look. Whenever I get a new project, I search my database of B contacts. Every time, I come up with at least a half dozen worth calling. Every time, at least one really helps with the project. And it's always fun."

"I don't have a database," Ben said.

"So do what Orville said. Go list some of them out. A hundred or two. Start a database."

"Okay," Ben agreed. "I don't know about a database and I'm still not so sure about that cheater Miles, but I'll work on my dormant contacts. When do I start contacting them? I'm ready to go."

"You have a Project Plan for your job search?" I asked.

"Of course. I read your other book. I'm all about Project Plans."

"How about telling us about it?" I suggested.

"Watch out, Ben," Rachel said, "He's checking your work. Get it right or he'll bench you."

"Nobody would bench a player who's as revved up as I am. But I gotta tell you, Coach," he said, looking at me, "that I have some doubts about the management part. I've done it but I don't always love it."

"I want him to stay with management," Jessie added, "It's like you said, Orville, straight engineering pays less."

"What about consulting?" I asked.

"Too much travel," Ben replied. "We'd rather take a short relocation if I can't find something right here. A 300 mile radius includes more than enough potential jobs."

"You should talk to consultants here at The Wall even though you're not going to be one." Rachel put in. "They know a lot of the right people all over the state."

"Thanks, Rachel," Ben replied. "I'd really like to do that. Can I call you tomorrow and talk about which ones and what they do?"

"Wow," I said, "You've been studying up, haven't you, Ben?"

"Yes," Rachel replied, "In the late afternoon would be good. And let's talk about Alicia, too."

"You have a Target List?" I asked

"Yes. It's at 53 organizations right now."

"Excellent. Do you want me to take a look at the whole plan?"

"I'd appreciate that. I'll e-mail it to you."

"Ben." Jessie said, "I have a couple of important additions for your Project Plan. Things you've missed."

"That's great," Ben said, taking the bait, "I am completely open to suggestions. What are they?"

"Clean the garage and fix that broken cabinet door."

**Use networking to create a
Project Plan for your job search.**

THEN USE NETWORKING TO:

Get your message out.

Gather information.

Meet insiders at targeted organizations.

Get in touch with Decision Makers.

| DECIDE | **PREPARE** | **TALK** | LAND |

Chapter Six

Plan Your Job Search— and Your Networking

Ask a job hunter what their plan is, and sometimes they'll look at you like you'd lost it. "Plan?" they say, "What do you mean, plan? My plan is to find a job."

Or they'll say, "My plan is to use the Internet." It's like asking someone the question, "What's your plan for building your new house?" And having them answer, "My plan is to use a hammer and saw." That's not a plan. That's a list of tools. A very short list.

On their last job, that same person always planned their projects carefully: goals, time required, resources, costs, contingencies, the whole works. But now, in job search, they seem to forget everything they know about organizing work. They act as if the search is something that's happening to them, something they have to cope with rather than something to plan and organize.

Happily, not everyone is like that. The best job hunters, of course, work this project in the same way they have always worked projects. Plan it, organize the work in some sensible way, implement in a disciplined manner, measure progress, and adjust plans as needed.

Networking can make your job hunting more effective. But of course networking is a tool, a process. Before we talk about the contribution networking can make, we need to talk about planning your job search. I consider this topic so important that I actually wrote four chapters on it—an approach called the Pierson Method—in another book, *The Unwritten Rules of the Highly Effective Job Search*.

There's no reason for you to drop this book and go read the other one right now. I'm going to give you a short version of the Pierson Method, starting right here so you can see how networking supports a well-planned highly effective search. If you have already read *The Unwritten Rules of the Highly Effective Job Search* and made a plan for your search, you can skip on ahead to the next main heading.

An Effective Project Plan Includes:

Professional Objective—What kind of work you want to do.

Target Market—Where you want to work.

Core Message—What you will say about yourself.

The first step in effective job hunting is to be clear about what you're hunting for. The more clearly you can state what kind of work you want, the easier it is to find it. You're not qualified for everything out there and there's a whole lot of jobs that you wouldn't want even if you could get them. The person who says, "I'll take anything," usually ends up with exactly that, just any old job—or worse, nothing. So starting out with a reasonable focus is important.

YOUR PROFESSIONAL OBJECTIVE

A Professional Objective defines what kind of work you want to do next. It tells employers what you're offering to do for them. It's usually a cluster of similar job titles. Most of us are qualified for multiple job titles, and different organizations sometimes put different titles on the same jobs.

There are a few titles—"accountant" for example—that are the same in virtually all organizations and exist in very large numbers. If you're in one of those categories, using the job title will work. But most of us need to figure out what the cluster is and label that cluster.

I like to call it Professional Objective, because what you're doing is first naming your profession and then labeling what you see as the best next step in that profession, your immediate objective. Please understand that the term "profession" is not limited to doctors, lawyers, teachers, and accountants. These days, any work based on a clearly defined body of knowledge and set of skills can be called a profession. So human resources, educational administration, computer programming, management, and sales can all be called professions. Here are some examples:

Senior Financial Executive

Human Resources Manager
Recruiting/Hiring…Compensation…Policies

Outside Sales

Administrative Assistant
Scheduling…Travel/Meeting Planning…
Spreadsheets/Databases

Notice that each names a profession and has a suggestion of level (for example, senior, manager, assistant). Some also suggest specific job functions that the job hunter wants as part of their next job (for example, compensation, scheduling).

If you have experience in a profession and are simply wanting to take the next step, stating a Professional Objective is usually not difficult. On the other hand, if you want to move to a new profession or if you're a recent graduate who has not yet become established in a profession, defining your Professional Objective may take more work. But the good news is that networking will help you get that work done.

Being able to state your Professional Objective is important because it focuses your search activities, enables other people to help you, and allows you to prepare a highly effective Core Message for use in resume writing and interviewing.

YOUR TARGET MARKET IS DEFINED BY LOCATION, INDUSTRY, AND SIZE

The second step in creating your Project Plan is determining your Target Market. In this part, I'm using language borrowed from the business discipline of marketing, because I think that's the most effective approach to this step. What you need to do is identify that group of potential employers most likely to hire someone with a Professional Objective like yours.

You're looking for employers who already have people working in the job titles that interest you. Don't worry about whether they have job openings or not. You're looking to make contact before the opening happens.

What's most important here is defining the kinds of organizations at which you most want to work. Look at the organizations that have the right jobs and narrow that list down to the ones you like the best. Then you can focus your networking on those organizations. This increases your chances of ending up working in a place you really like.

For some people, it makes more sense to determine Target Market before thinking about Professional Objective. Recent college grads and people considering a major career change are sometimes in this category. If you go this way, find several organizations you like. Then look to see what they have in common, so you can expand the list even further with additional similar organizations. As you do that, begin looking to see what their job titles are and which are best suited for you.

In determining your Target Market, the first step is defining the geographic area where you want to work. It's important to define it precisely enough that you can draw it on a map. If it's about a commuting range, it might look like a big amoeba, reaching out farther in directions where the commute is easier.

Usually the best way to define it is by city, county, or postal code, because these can be used in most databases. Sometimes the same job is different in different locations. Teaching high school biology in a poor New York City neighborhood, for example, is a different job from a high school biology teacher in a wealthy Chicago suburb.

If a relocation might be needed, select one or more alternate locations, defining each in the same way. Prioritize these, so you'll spend the most job-hunting time on the geographic areas where you most want to live. That way, you maximize your chances of living there. And, of course, you put no effort at all into places that you dislike.

Next comes defining the type of organization you're looking for. For example, is it a governmental organization, a business, an educational organization, or not-for-profit? If it's government, is it federal, state, or local? Which government agency? If it's a business, what industries do you prefer? Manufacturing? Healthcare? Insurance? There are dozens to choose from. If it's an educational organization you want, is it public or private? Elementary? Secondary? A university? You need to define your ideal organization. The more precisely you define it, the better. And of course, you can simultaneously pursue more than one kind of organization.

Along with geographic location and type of organization, you also need to decide the size of the organization. Would you rather be part of an organization with 10 employees? 100 employees? 1,000? 10,000? If it's a business, do you want to work for a business with $1 million in annual revenue or $1 billion? Please notice that the same job title can be very different in different sized organizations.

For example, an accountant working in an organization of 100 probably has a very different job from an accountant who is one of 10,000 employees. An HR Director for 1,000 employees has a different job from one with 50,000 employees. A Chief Executive Officer for a business under $1 million might sweep the floor and take out the trash. A CEO in a business of more than $500 million has a very different job—and a very different paycheck.

Define a size range either by annual revenue or by number of employees. Then use that size range as one of the criteria for your Target List.

YOUR TARGET LIST IS JUST AS IMPORTANT AS YOUR RESUME

Once you have determined those three parts of your Target Market—geographic location, type of organization, and size—you can use them to create an actual Target List of employers you want to work for. Having a written Target List is just as important as having a resume. Both are essential tools in an effective search.

There are numerous directories and databases that will help you create a Target List once you have defined the three criteria: geographic location, type of organization, and size. With a database, you can enter the three criteria, and the database will compile your list.

Without a database, you'll browse through printed directories. These books use the same three criteria, and the browsing will allow you to screen the organizations as you create the list.

If you don't know where to find these directories and databases, ask a reference librarian in the biggest and best library you can find. Be sure to tell that person that you are interested in researching organizations, not job openings. For most job hunters, a list of 40 to 50 organizations is a good starting point.

When you're doing this research, make sure your Target List is large enough that there are likely to be enough jobs coming open each month during your job search. You can do this by estimating the total number of jobs in each organization and estimating the turnover in those jobs. It's nearly impossible to get precise information on either of these. But guesstimates are good enough for what we're doing here.

For example, if there were 48 salespeople in an organization and their average tenure was four years, then you could expect that organization to have 12 openings a year or one a month. If you're a CEO, then there's only one job per organization, and you'll need more organizations on your list than the salesperson.

In defining your Target Market, you're defining your personal job market—the group of organizations where you're going to focus your efforts in job search. It's important to make sure the market you define is big enough. I like to see an estimated 10 to 50 jobs coming open each month in a job hunter's personal job market.

If there is any doubt about whether your personal job market is big enough, please enlarge it immediately. Pursuing an unrealistically small market is a common reason why searches fail to produce results, especially in higher level managerial and executive jobs.

If your personal job market comes out too small on the first try, enlarge it by expanding the geographic area you're covering, enlarging your Professional Objective to include more job titles, or expanding the size or industry range you first used.

YOUR CORE MESSAGE DESCRIBES YOUR QUALIFICATIONS IN THE LANGUAGE OF YOUR TARGET MARKET

The third and last part of your Project Plan is your Core Message. This is the message you want to deliver to Decision Makers in your personal job market. It tells them how very useful you'll be when you work for them. Your most effective way of getting this message to potential employers is networking. And, of course, the same message is contained in your resume.

Many people believe that writing a resume is the first step in job hunting. In fact, you'll write a much better resume once you're clear on your Professional Objective and Target Market. After all, the resume is all about telling a particular group of people (your Target Market) how effective you are doing a particular kind of work (your Professional Objective).

In writing your resume, always ask whether the Decision Makers in your chosen Target Market will like what you're saying. These are the readers who matter the most. Other people's opinions on your resume don't matter nearly as much.

Your Core Message is not just about your resume. In a job search, you need to talk about yourself frequently and to many people. You'll use your Core Message with recruiters, in interviewing, and throughout the networking process. Because you will be saying the same thing over and over, it's well worth taking the time to compose the most effective possible message. The verbal version of it is much shorter than your resume. You need to be able to deliver it in two minutes or less.

This is very important, so I'll say it once more. Your Core Message tells your Target Market how effective you will be in doing the work described by your Professional Objective. Plan it carefully. It will make your networking more productive.

YOUR PROJECT PLAN PREPARES YOU FOR A PROACTIVE JOB SEARCH

Once you have a Project Plan (Professional Objective, Target Market, and Core Message) and a Target List, you're ready to launch a proactive and highly effective job search. In fact, you may want to begin your search before those pieces are completed, because networking produces job market information that will help you complete the Project Plan. And networking is always an important part of building and refining a Target List.

If you accidentally find a job while you're still working on refining your plan and list, that's great! That kind of thing does happen, and it's not really an accident. It's the result of your good work (plus maybe some good luck). It's the way the Pierson Method works.

But, in case you haven't gotten that offer just yet, let's look at exactly how to use networking in creating a great job-search Project

Plan. The two places where networking helps most are your Professional Objective and your Target List.

Use Networking to:

Create and Refine Your Professional Objective

For recent graduates and job hunters considering a major career change, creating a Professional Objective can require a great deal of thought. If you're in this category, I'd like to suggest that in addition to thinking about your Professional Objective, you take three other steps that will speed the process.

First, you might want to read some books on making career choices. My first book has a chapter on the topic, and I've listed some others for you on my Website, highlyeffectivejobsearch.com. Career planning books will help you establish a roadmap for your career and provide useful approaches to the career decision-making process.

Personally, I favor a career planning process that begins with imagining or envisioning—in a total "blue sky" manner—what kind of work you would like to do. When you have an idea or two, collect the real-world information that will enable you to decide whether you would like *doing* that work as much as you like imagining it. Also, gather information that will tell you whether you are currently qualified for that kind of work—and if not, what you would need to do to become qualified. So step two is reading and Internet research on kinds of work that attract you.

Step three, as you've surely guessed, is networking. Networking is the single best way to find out what a job entails, what skills are required, and everything else you need to know about the job to decide if you want it and what you'd need to do in order to get it. There's no substitute for talking to someone who actually has that job title or has held it in the past.

As I've mentioned, doing this kind of thing is sometimes called "information interviewing." This actually goes beyond networking because you're asking someone you may not know very well to spend 30 minutes, an hour, or more with you and to provide a great deal of information. You can use networking to locate the right person, someone likely to respond positively to your request for this kind of assistance.

This approach is commonly used by recent graduates and career changers. When handled appropriately, it works very well. The key to making it work is your clear and honest interest in the kind of work you are exploring—as well as your prior thought, research, and preparation of questions.

Refining a Professional Objective is easier than creating one at the beginning of a career. It's something you can do all along the way in your normal networking. It's a natural part of conversations with peers, people who are currently holding jobs similar to the one you're looking for. If you are not making a major career change, you have many shared interests with people in the jobs defined by your Professional Objective because you've been in that kind of work yourself. It's easy to compare notes, asking your peers how their current job differs from your current or last job and how they are the same.

What you are doing in this case is better understanding the differences between similar job titles. This will enable you to see whether your Professional Objective might be more effective if it was a bit broader, narrower, or focused in a slightly different way.

This kind of networking conversation has an added advantage: it allows people to see and understand your qualifications. People who currently hold job titles that you are interested in are people who report to Decision Makers who could be your next boss. If they see you as qualified, they may very well pass that information on to the Decision Maker.

Use Networking to:

Create and Refine Your Target List

If you are planning to continue in the same kind of work you have been doing, you can probably name several desirable employers right now. This is a great way to get your Target List started, but it's also important that you go beyond these obvious choices to create the best Target List possible.

You should definitely do the research we discussed earlier in this chapter. Go to a library and use the geographic location, industry, and size criteria from the Target Market part of your Project Plan to create a more extensive list. Organize that list into categories. If you are pursuing more than one industry, those are the most logical categories to use. But you can break the list into any logical categories. The point is simply to make the list easier to browse by breaking it into sections, just as I did with the Mapping Your Networks list on page 90.

Your Target List is an excellent tool to use in networking with your friends and acquaintances. Show them the list. Ask them if they would be comfortable discussing it with you. Be sure that they understand that you are looking for information about the organizations, and do not expect to locate immediate job openings. Ask them if they've heard of any of the organizations on your list. If so, talk about those and find out what they know. Use this information to help decide whether to advance an organization to the top of your priority list—or perhaps drop it completely.

Don't forget to ask your networking partners if they have suggestions for organizations to add to the list or suggestions about which organizations should be deleted. You can also ask which of the categories they think are best for you. In all of these cases, ask why. The "why" information is usually the most useful of all.

With people you know less well, you may not show them the list, but you can nonetheless mention some of the organizations by name in conversation. Whenever the topic of your job search comes up, it's easy and logical to mention a few organizations you are interested in to see if your networking partner knows anything about them.

The work of refining your Target List continues throughout your search. You get information that you need to refine your list by networking. Having a list makes networking easier, because talking about organizations is an easy and comfortable topic in casual conversation. We'll discuss all of this further in Chapter Seven, Your Personal Networks and How to Use Them.

Once your Project Plan is completed, you're ready to begin pursuing the goals we discussed in Chapter Two: get the word out, gather information, meet insiders, and get in touch with Decision Makers. These goals are designed to move you step by step closer to your next job. The remainder of this chapter looks at how to use networking to achieve these goals.

Use Networking to:

Get Your Message Out

Another reason you created your Project Plan—Professional Objective, Target Market, and Core Message—is because that is exactly the information that you want to get out to people on your network. Networks, of course, are a way to spread information as well as to collect it. When people say, "I heard it through the grapevine," that's what they're talking about: information moving on networks.

The most important information you want to spread on your networks is the combination of your Professional Objective (the kind of work you're looking for) and your Core Message (why you're a good candidate for that kind of work). The more people who know this, the more likely it is that a Decision Maker will hear about it. Along with your Professional Objective and Core Message, you want everyone to know is that you are currently *available*.

Getting your message out is a bit delicate if you are currently employed. The more people who know about your availability, the faster your search goes. However, the more of this information that gets back to your current boss, the better your chances of earning a spot on the layoff list. So exercise caution and get started with your personal—rather than professional—networks.

The rewards of getting your message out effectively can be significant. Its not uncommon for career consultants to hear from job hunters who say, "I got a call out of the blue, a request for an interview from a Decision Maker I never met." When that happens, it's usually not out of the blue at all, it's because the job hunter got the message out.

Use Networking to:

Gather Information

It is said that knowledge is power. Well, knowledge certainly is one of the things that gives you power in your job search. We discussed gathering information to create and refine a Target List. You'll also network to research individual targets and take a broader look at your personal job market. Both of these provide information that will be useful in selecting the best targets, gaining entrance to them, and making the best impression when you get there.

RESEARCH INDIVIDUAL TARGETS

You will be using your Target List throughout your job search. For most people, a list of 40 to 50 targeted organizations is about right. But the higher your compensation, the longer a list you are likely to need. A senior executive might have a list of 100. Although the list may stay about the same length throughout your search, its contents will change as you eliminate some organizations and add others.

No matter how long your list is, you will always prioritize it. Each week, you want to focus your efforts on the best organizations on your Target List. Of course it's up to you to decide which are the best. Your criteria might include its reputation in the industry, its location, how it compensates people, how successful it is, what its culture and values are, or anything else that's important to you. Consider your criteria early in your search and refine them as you go.

In order to prioritize your list, you need to have information on each organization. An obvious and important first step is to check the Website. See how the organization is described, who they are, and howthey are doing. Then, while your computer is still turned on, Google it. The Website told you what its people think about the organization. Googling them tells you what other people have to say about them. If you're a manager, look to see who the top executives are and Google those people too.

But please don't spend all day staring at a computer screen. Networking—talking to people, not sitting at the computer—is what is going to get you there. And, as you know, networking is by far the best source of information about any organization. The most important information is not on the Internet and is not published anywhere.

You will get your very best information by talking to people who have had personal experience of any kind with the organization: former employees, vendors, customers, clients, or consultants are all great. Of course, the *most* useful thing you can do is talk to someone who works there right now. If they're in the right job title or the right departments, that's even better. But anyone who works there probably knows more than you do. So talk to as many people as you can.

SURVEY YOUR PROFESSION AND INDUSTRY

When beginning a job search, it's smart to take a look around and see what's going on in your profession in other organizations. If you're a member of a professional organization and have been doing that all along, congratulations. That's great career management, and it's an advantage if you have already done that on the day you begin job hunting.

But if you haven't joined a professional organization yet, don't worry. It's easy to combine professional development with the rest of your networking. The issue here is very simple: you want to be sure that you are up-to-date professionally. The more up-to-date you are, the more aware you are of the latest innovations and trends, and the more appealing you will be as a candidate.

The same is true of industry. The more you know about what's going on in the industries or types of organizations that you're interested in, the more appealing a candidate you become. This is true for everyone, but especially true for managers and executives. You need to know what's going on and people need to see that you know that.

There's a second advantage here. The more you find out about what's going on in your profession and industry, the more interesting you are as a networking partner when talking to professional contacts. You have useful information to share with your peers.

If you're a recent grad or a career changer, professional and industry information are even more important, and both should be collected early in your search. It's important for you to be sure that you are interested in the industries and types of organizations you plan to pursue. You also need to learn to speak the language of the industry and the profession. Each has its own jargon, and the more you are familiar with it, the more you sound interested and knowledgeable, like someone who has done their homework.

Surveying a profession and choosing a Professional Objective, of course, go hand in hand. For a recent grad or career changer, the two are part of the same process of making career decisions. For anyone, professional information is valuable in job-search networking.

Use Networking to:

Meet Insiders at Targeted Organizations

In talking to people about your Target List and individual targets, it's not difficult to locate people currently employed at some of those targets. After all, you have a lot of organizations on your Target List. If you are talking to someone who lives in the geographic area where your targets are located or knows that area, the odds are actually in your favor. And if you are actively inquiring about people as well as other information, you will certainly be able to get some names.

Of course, you won't talk to every person you hear of. You want your networking partners to make introductions only when they believe that you and the other person will enjoy meeting each other. Or at least that the two of you will be likely to have a comfortable conversation.

In the course of your job hunting, it's entirely possible that you will meet some people whom you like a lot. Some of them may become professional colleagues or long-term members of your professional network. Some might even become friends. And, of course, you'll also have some conversations that go nowhere at all.

If you have the good fortune to strike up a positive relationship with an insider at one of your targeted organizations, that person may take an active interest in bringing you into the organization. In some organizations, employees actually get a cash bonus for bringing in job candidates who are later hired. Even without a bonus, an insider may decide that they would really like to have a person like you for a colleague.

In this case, they might introduce you to other employees, provide you with useful information about the organization and its hiring process, and introduce you to the Decision Maker. If it doesn't occur to them to do these things, it's okay with me if you decide to ask.

Use Networking to:

Get in Touch With Decision Makers

I hope that you've noticed by now how there can be a natural, easy flow in job-search networking. You talk to people about what kind of work you want to do and where you want to do it. Those conversations include discussion of specific organizations. In discussing organizations, you sometimes move to talking about people who work for them. You look for opportunities to meet those Insiders. You make sure they have the right information about you. You ask for an introduction to the Decision Maker.

None of this is about job openings. Effective job hunters usually meet the Decision Maker before there is a job opening—or at least before the Decision Maker is willing to talk about an upcoming opening. Because you'd prefer to work upstream of the openings, you look to meet the right Decision Makers whenever you can do that, regardless of openings.

Because there is no opening, this meeting with the Decision Maker will not be a job interview. In fact, it might just be an opportunity to say hello to that person while visiting with another employee. If you're able to mention your interest in working for the organization, that's a good thing. If you're able to mention a few of your qualifications, that's even better.

But the central point here is this: Most job hunters are hired by Decision Makers whom they met informally before the opening happened.

Job hunters usually have conversations with numerous Decision Makers on the way to being hired by one of them. The more Decision Makers you talk to, the more the odds tilt in your favor that one will have an opening soon. Most of these conversations are not interviews. They're informal. They can be on the phone or in person. They might be two hours at lunch or two minutes standing in a hallway.

The way you are most likely to have those informal conversations with Decision Makers is by systematically networking from people you know to Insiders at your targets to the Decision Makers. In fact, that's how millions of people find jobs.

Moving From Preparation Into Broader Networking

Preparation is an important part of success in any work project. The most important preparation in job hunting is making a Project Plan: deciding what you want to do (your Professional Objective), where you want to do it (your Target Market and Target List), and how you will present yourself on a resume and informally when you talk to people (your Core Message). The most important products of your preparation are your Target List and resume.

Early networking is part of completing this preparation and checking to see that it's done in the most effective way possible. Information you get from other people will help you prepare for all aspects of your search project. This initial networking is usually limited to an inner circle of people you know and trust. Some of them may serve as a sounding board, or even become an informal board of advisors. In other words, it all starts with personal contacts.

After your preparation is completed, networking can get you inside the right organizations, talking to the right people. It can get your message out broadly enough that information and opportunities start coming your way.

In this chapter, we have completed the "Prepare" part of the Decide-Prepare-Talk-Land sequence and begun the "Talk" portion. In the next chapter, we'll continue with "Talk" by taking a careful look at networking with your personal contacts.

ORVILLE'S JOURNAL

Hitting the Wall, Joining the Team, and Getting Things Moving

"Where have you been, Ben?" I asked. I hadn't seen him for nearly two weeks. But now he and Jessie were sitting on the sofa in my office.

"I hit a rough spot, coach," he replied, sipping his herbal tea.

"That's the understatement of the year," Jessie added, "He went charging out of our last meeting and hit the wall at 70 miles per hour. Then he was depressed for a week. It isn't going to be like this the whole time, is it Orville?"

"I wasn't depressed. Not all week. I slacked off, I admit. But I had to think things over."

"Why didn't you stop by?" I asked, "Or at least send me an e-mail?"

"I didn't want to bother you, Orville."

"Hey, it's my job. I'm your coach, remember? And a friend, too, I hope."

"Okay, I was a little discouraged. I called my best contacts and nothing happened with any of them. Eight people. No results."

"They were all management contacts," Jessie put in. "None were hiring. They didn't know of any openings. Three of them didn't return his phone call."

"Ah," I said, "You were maybe trying to skip some steps and make a quick leap into a job?"

"Yeah," he replied, "And it didn't work. So now I'm back reading your book. I think I see where I went wrong. I should have started with Rachel's friends and Jessie's friends. And my real friends, not just the higher-ups I know."

"I agree that you should always start with the easy ones," I said, "but you have to figure out who the easy ones are."

"That's exactly what his job hunting team said," Jessie put in. "He finally went over to the church and joined the team."

"How's that going?" I asked.

"Great." Ben smiled for the first time. "They started by asking to see my Target List. Six of them had information about targets. I got the names of four new targets. One is a company 12 miles from here that I had never heard of before."

"It's easier with your team members," I volunteered. "They understand how to do a good search. You don't have to explain it."

"And the thing about networking inside a community makes it easier too," Jessie added. "When Ben came back from his team meeting, he was a new man."

"Teams aren't the only way to do it," I said, "You can do exactly the same thing with other contacts. You just need to learn how."

"I know. I'm starting to get it. I had lunch with Alicia. That was easy too. Fun, actually."

"What happened?"

"Rachel's right, Orville. Alicia's great. You should meet her too. She's got this amazing project searching eight global databases for information that will confirm a theory on organizational behavior. She's going to change the field of management."

"So what happened?"

Ben looked confused.

"Your job search, Ben." Jessie smiled. "Orville doesn't care about anything but job hunting. Tell him that part."

I nodded. "Having a great conversation and finding more common interests is the perfect way to start. But you went farther than that, right?"

"Right. I told her how I was doing my job search, explained my Project Plan and all that. She looked at the Target List and gave me six names right off the bat. People to talk to. I was amazed. Two are in manufacturing. One is an engineering professor at State. She's a sociologist. I didn't think that would happen."

"Well, it doesn't always."

"Yeah, I know. I talked to four people my team introduced me to that went no place at all. Nice friendly talk, but no information, no introductions. Nothing."

"Yet," Jessie added.

"Yes, I suppose something could come of it. I gave them all my Target List. I'll be talking to them again."

"You're off to a great start," I said. "You've read the chapter on personal contacts?"

"Yes and professional contacts, too. I think I see how it all fits together. And I'm starting to figure out what to say."

"I think not knowing what to say was the problem with those managers," Jessie suggested.

"Yeah," Ben said, "You're right. I took them on too soon. I didn't know what to say. I blew it."

"It's not over yet," I put in. "You can go back and talk to them again."

"Yes, and I think I know why those three didn't return my phone call. It was the voicemail I left. But you're right. I can circle back to them. And I will. After I do some more personal contacts and a little more research."

"Good. Can we talk again in a week? I'm glad you're on a team, but I'm still your coach and I want to make sure you keep on building momentum."

"Yes," Ben said. "I'd like to do that."

Jessie looked at me, then at Ben. "Good," she said. "That way maybe I won't have to drag you out from under the bed anymore."

Networking with Your Personal Contacts

Make your networking partner comfortable.

Get your message out.

Gather information to refine and expand your Target List.

Get introductions to new personal and professional contacts.

| DECIDE | PREPARE | **TALK** | LAND |

Chapter Seven

Your Personal Networks and How to Use Them

If I could give only one sentence of advice to job hunters, it would be: "Talk with as many people as possible about your job search."

If your job search is like most, talking to people is the most important thing you can do. If you're smart about who you talk to and what you say, your search will go faster and better. But even if you're not very smart about it—even if you don't think about it very much or plan it very well—you will still find a job, if only you hang in there, keep at it, and listen as well as talk.

This chapter is about talking with people and listening to what they have to say. In particular, it's about talking with people who are members of your personal networks, people you are already connected with in one way or another. There will be a lot of suggestions— all based on my experience working with job hunters and career consultants—of what works well and what does not, and a number of scripts to suggest words you might use.

I hope and expect that you will find many of the ideas in this chapter useful. But I also expect that you'll find some ideas and suggestions that simply don't work for you. Everyone is different, and everyone's networks are different. So please take what works and leave the rest. And remember, the single most important thing is to talk with people about your job search—the more people the better—and listen to them too.

In all of your networking conversations, I hope you'll remember those four networking goals we talked about in Chapter Two. You are networking to get the word out about you and your job search, to gather information that will make your search more effective, to talk to Insiders at your targeted organizations, and finally, to get in touch with Decision Makers.

In order to achieve these goals, it's good to have a plan and to work on it systematically, remembering our discussions about networks, networking, and how it all works. It's also important to remember that most people need to proceed step-by-step in job-search networking. With your personal networks, you're working on the first two of those goals, and getting the word out and gathering information. You are also setting yourself up for the other two, talking to Insiders, and getting in touch with Decision Makers.

There's a tendency for job hunters to want to jump immediately to the fourth goal, skipping goals one through three. They get impatient. They want to talk to Decision Makers immediately. They want interviews and offers right now. So they set networking aside and put too much time into less effective methods that seem more direct.

I certainly don't blame anyone for being in a hurry, especially if they're unemployed. But for most people, talking to personal contacts does not produce interviews or job offers. Most people find jobs at the second or third degree of separation, not the first.

So with personal contacts, the first degree of separation, you're looking to get your message out, gather information to refine your Target List, and get introductions to those Insiders and Decision Makers you want to meet. Then, armed with great information, you move to the second and third degrees of separation and talk to professional contacts.

CONFIDANTES AND BROADER PERSONAL NETWORKS

More often than not, you'll need to do the early steps in order to get to the later ones. You start at the first degree of separation, then move to the next. Sometimes you can skip a step, but other times trying to skip a step—like leaping to a new contact without an introduction from an existing contact—can actually take you backward. Most of the time, it's easier and more effective to find an introduction than to make a cold contact.

For most people, the initial steps are all about talking to people they already know very well. If you have doubts or problems about your job search, it's sometimes very useful to talk those over with other people. At the same time, when you're in a job search you don't want to spread negative information about yourself. You want other people to talk about you, but those conversations need to be positive conversations that will help you get a new job.

So my suggestion is to select a few people—perhaps just one—for coaching, advice, and problem-solving. Share everything in confidence with this little group and don't put the difficult, negative, or problematic conversations out there on your broader networks.

Remember, one of your goals here is to get your message out on all of the appropriate networks. The message you want to get out is about your availability to do certain kinds of work in certain organizations and your ability to do that work well. Your enthusiasm about the work and the organizations that you are pursuing is an important part of being successful. Getting negative information out there on the grapevine will just slow you down.

So be careful who you talk to about your last employer's faults, how much you dislike your current job, how tough your job search is, or how many doubts you have about where your career is going. Save that for those very few people you trust to keep it to themselves.

As for your broader networking, we'll get started right now by looking at your personal networks. We will particularly look at people you have personal relationships with and people who are members of the same communities you are. In other words, we'll start with the people who are easiest for you to talk to. I'm going to divide these people into three groups, or concentric circles that surround you.

Your Personal Contacts: You Have Common Interests With All of Them

Inner Circle—strong relationships, community connections.

Middle Circle—casual relationships, community connections.

Outer Circle—dormant and passive connections, possible community connections.

Your Inner Circle includes those people you talk to all the time. They're friends, acquaintances, and relatives. They are one degree of separation from you. They are easy to talk to. There is a strong relationship or a strong community connection or both.

Your Middle Circle includes people you have personal and community relationships with, but those relationships aren't quite as strong. You do talk to these people, but not as often. Like your Inner Circle, they are also one degree of separation from you.

The relationships we're talking about here are personal, not professional, so people you know from past employment are not included here, unless they are also personal friends. (We'll deal with professional contacts in the next chapter.)

Your Outer Circle of personal contacts includes dormant and passive networking connections, such as the college classmate whom you never met or the one whom you haven't talked to in years. These are people you have some kind of personal connection with. It may not be a strong one. Nonetheless, they are only one degree of separation from you, and it's good to remember Granovetter's famous statement about how strong weak connections can be.

Your Personal Contacts	
Inner Circle: Active Contacts. Strong shared interests, relationships, or community connections.	Talk in depth to all of them.
Middle Circle: Shared interests, casual relationships, community connections.	Talk to most of these—some in depth, some more briefly.
Outer Circle: Dormant or passive contacts. Shared interests, possible community connections.	Be selective with this large group. Look for multiple shared interests, community connections, and dormant relationships that were once strong.

Your goals for networking conversations with people in these three circles are the same, but how you pursue those goals will be a little different with each. Let's take a look at the goals.

Networking With Your Personal Contacts

· **Make your networking partner comfortable.**
· **Get the word out.**
· **Gather information to refine and expand your Target List.**
· **Get introductions to new personal and professional contacts.**

It's a good idea to have goals in all of your networking conversations. With personal contacts, you are dealing with friends, so the conversations don't need to be formal. There's a social aspect, and you might enjoy the process.

At the same time, highly effective job hunting is a work project and you need to stay focused in order to get the work done. So I think it's good to be clear on your goals before any networking conversation, even one with a friend.

As we've mentioned, your four networking goals are getting the word out, gathering information, talking to Insiders, and getting in touch with Decision Makers. With your personal contacts, you are working on the first two. At the same time, you're laying the groundwork for success in the third and fourth goals by gathering information and getting introductions.

In order to be effective, you will *always* need to make your networking partners comfortable. But you don't need to accomplish all of the other three items on the list on page 137 in every conversation. Whenever you accomplish any of those three, you have had a great conversation. If you accomplish more than one of them, that's outstanding.

Getting your message out and gathering information are central job-hunting goals, and if you accomplish either of those, you had a great conversation. The same is true of refining and expanding your Target List: if that's all you accomplish, you had a great conversation. And of course, new introductions are what keeps your job search moving and expanding.

A meeting where you got a new introduction and nothing else would be a great meeting. The more introductions you can get to new professional contacts, the faster your search moves. But first and always, it's about comfortable conversations.

Make Your Networking Partner Comfortable

Clear up myths and misunderstandings.
Tell them what you want and don't want.
Tell the truth.
Express your gratitude.

Your first goal in any networking meeting with any networking partner is always making that person comfortable throughout the entire conversation. This is a goal you should work to achieve in every single conversation in your search because it's important to protect your reputation and keep your networking moving. Remember, some of your networking partners have probably had bad experiences with job hunters who network poorly.

Most job hunters use networking, or at least try to use it. There are many books and Websites that recommend job-search networking and suggest all kinds of different ways of doing it. It looks to me like some of the suggested networking methods are too aggressive—and sometimes even offensive.

I sometimes talk to people who feel like they've been "networked to death" by job hunters who don't do it very well. Sometimes I even hesitate to use the word networking, because it generates such mixed reactions.

I often prefer to say that the whole thing is just about "talking to people." And that might be a good way for you to discuss it as well. When you do your job-search networking in a skilled and sensitive way, people sometimes will not label it as networking at all. They'll just see it as "talking to you about your job hunting." Or as having a chat with a friend.

There are several reasons why people are sometimes uncomfortable networking with job hunters. First, they might be uncomfortable because they believe some of those myths we talked about in Chapter Three. For example, if someone believes that they are expected to introduce you to Mr. Bigshot, that could make them uncomfortable—whether they know Mr. B or not. Sometimes it's a good idea to explicitly reassure people that you are not asking for any big, impossible favors.

Oddly enough, personal contacts are sometimes uncomfortable because they want so badly to help you. When they think of job hunting, most people think of job openings. Whether you ask them about job openings or not, they may believe that telling you about job openings is the only way they can help you. But it's almost certain that they don't know of any job openings appropriate for you. They really want to help, but they're convinced that they can't. It looks impossible. It makes them feel inadequate and uncomfortable.

If you're unemployed while job hunting, that can make people even more uncomfortable, especially if you have dependents. They might think, "Oh my goodness, she's a single mom with no job. What if she runs out of money?" Or, "Wow, he has three dependants and no income!" Then they want even more to help and feel even more uncomfortable.

Another reason for discomfort is this: People who have had bad experiences with job hunters might worry that you are going to be pushy and try to get them to do things they don't want to do. In other words, they might be expecting you to behave like an overly aggressive used car salesperson. Then their defenses are up and they're uncomfortable throughout the conversation, just waiting for you to "put the squeeze on them."

The simplest way to make your personal contacts comfortable is to tell them the exact truth. Tell them at the very outset what you have in mind and what your goals are in the conversation. Explain how you're doing job hunting, and which steps you're working on right now.

Perhaps most important, it helps to tell them what you don't want and what you don't expect. For example, it is sometimes important to tell people that you would be grateful to have introductions to other people but *only* if they believe that you and the new person will get along well—and *only* if they're comfortable making the introduction.

There are any number of additional ways that you can make people comfortable. One is simply expressing your gratitude, especially for those little things that help move your job search a step or two along the way. Sometimes people don't understand how useful a piece of information about a target can be, or an introduction to someone inside a target.

A thank you, an e-mailed or handwritten note, or sometimes even a little token thank you gift can go a long way with a personal contact. Sometimes asking your networking partner to share their own experiences at work or in job hunting opens up a rich conversation that both of you will enjoy. And, as we'll discuss in Chapter Nine, keeping people informed is a networking courtesy that works well with all contacts.

Throughout this chapter, I'll give you suggested scripts. These are examples of how you might express some of these ideas in real conversations, and in ways that people are likely to be comfortable with. Please feel free to take whatever phrases and sentences work for you and use them.

Get Your Message Out

Tell everyone about your Professional Objective, Target Market, and Core Message.

Getting your message out is like planting seeds, so plant a lot of them.

I've said it before, but it's worth saying again. Telling people about your job search is a very effective way of finding a new job. Much of this book is about collecting information, but spreading information is also important. The more people who know what kind of work you seek, what kind of organizations you are interested in, and what your relevant skills and talents are, the better your chances are.

This isn't about telling everyone, "I'm looking for a job with good advancement possibilities at a dynamic growing company." That kind of statement is worthless. It doesn't say anything. It certainly doesn't give anyone any way that they can help. You need to tell your personal network contacts the basics of the Project Plan we discussed on page 112 of Chapter Six:

> **Your Professional Objective,** or what kind(s) of work you're interested in.
>
> **Your Target Market,** or the kinds of organizations where you'd like to work.

Your Core Message, or the three most important reasons why that kind of organization might be interested in you for that kind of work.

It's important to formulate these three carefully, so your listeners understand what you're doing in your job search. You need to be able to cover all three areas in 30 seconds or less, though a more detailed two-minute version is also useful with people who want to know more. If you later show the same people your Target List, it will help them understand your Target Market even better.

If you're unsure of any of these three areas, keep your networking more limited until you've figured them out and made the appropriate decisions. Then begin your broader networking.

Early in any conversation with a personal network contact, you need to tell your networking partner these three things. It's information they need in order to understand what you're up to and in order to help you.

And it might not be just you that they are helping. Remember that people who pass on information about you to potential employers are also doing the employer a favor by enabling the Decision Maker to have access to a good candidate without spending any money to do it.

All in all, I'd say that getting your message out is like planting seeds. You should do it in every networking conversation, and even in conversations that you do not consider to be networking. You should also ask your friends to do it on your behalf. Plant enough seeds, and some will produce offers of information. Plant enough seeds, and one of them will sprout into an invitation to interview.

My wife, Judy, once did this kind of thing inadvertently. Here's what happened.

Once I was on a business trip, and I brought her a souvenir coffee mug from Singapore. She liked it, so I started getting her mugs whenever I saw a nice one. When we went on family vacations, she picked up mugs from places we visited. Judy served coffee in these interesting unmatched mugs, so people began seeing her mug collection.

She was a high school guidance counselor, so she visited colleges that her high school students might want to attend. She got mugs from the colleges too, and kept them in her office at school.

Soon, the word was out, and I wasn't the only person giving her mugs. She began to get gifts of all kind of coffee mugs from all kinds of people. We bought a display cabinet to put them in. When the collection topped 300 mugs, we gave quite a number away. But to this day, we have a cabinet full of fascinating coffee mugs.

The same kind of thing can happen to you in your job search. Get the message out about what you're interested in, and information will start coming your way, just like the coffee mugs came Judy's way. It takes a little time to get it started. But once you do, it can turn into a small tsunami of information. Information is an easy gift to give someone, even easier than a coffee mug.

NETWORKING WHILE EMPLOYED

I am well aware that spreading this kind of message about your job search broadly is risky for people who are currently employed. If you're in that group, you should put particular emphasis on personal contacts.

Your personal contacts are usually the lowest risk. You should work those networks as thoroughly as possible, and be careful about how and when you move to professional networking—where there's a higher likelihood of it getting back to your current boss.

You can reduce the risk by talking to professional contacts about how you'd like to "one day" move to another kind of work (name it) or another kind of employer (name it). This is usually enough to get the message across. You can make stronger statements to people you trust and you can "reluctantly" accept offers to interviews.

If confronted by your current employer, remember that while they may have some information about your job hunting, they certainly don't know everything. So don't make any big confessions. If necessary, you can admit to "always keeping your eyes open for future possibilities." But don't complain about your current job or employer. Doing so is poor career management for anyone and particularly risky for people conducting a job search. So get your message out, but do it with caution.

Gather Information to Refine and Expand Your Target List

Get the list up to 40 or 50 organizations.
Gather information to prioritize the list.
Explain what you are doing and why.

When approached in the right way, networking partners are almost always comfortable sharing information. After all, information exchange is what real networking is about.

Information is at the heart of a highly effective job search. After all, this is the Information Age. Having the right information is the key to getting almost anything done and job hunting is no exception.

If you're at entry level or making a major career change, your first and largest information need might be the information that helps you decide exactly which groups of jobs to go after, what your Professional Objective should be. In this case, you might be networking with your Inner Circle primarily to locate information on particular jobs and careers.

Anyone in a job search should be creating a Target List and gathering information about organizations on that list. With each organization, you are making an educated guess that they employ people in the job titles you're looking for. If you're not sure, put them on your list and find out through your networking.

For most people, 40 to 50 organizations is about the right length for a Target List. If you're having trouble getting that many, start networking with your Inner Circle and see if they can help you expand the list.

Ask people in your Inner Circle if they would be willing to take a look at your list and discuss it with you. You can do the same with many of your Middle Circle contacts, as well. When one of your networking partners is looking at the list, ask them questions like these:

- *Are you familiar with any of these organizations?*

- *I'd be very interested to hear anything you know about that organization.*

- *Based on what I told you about my Project Plan for job hunting, which of these organizations do you think would be most appropriate for me? Why?*

- *Can you think of any organizations I should add to my list? Why do you suggest that one?*

- *Are there any organizations you think I should remove from the list? Why?*

- *Are you aware of any directories, Websites, or databases that I could use to locate additional organizations like these?*

- *Do you know anyone else who might be able to help me refine and expand this list?*

These and other questions like them are designed to open a conversation with your networking partner that will help you refine your Target List. In that discussion, you may spend a great deal of time discussing a particular organization that your networking partner knows well. Sometimes you'll get so much information that you'll want to take notes on it.

To go into greater depth on one particular organization, you might want to ask questions such as:

- *What are their goals, and what are they trying to accomplish?*

- *What successes have they had recently?*

- *Have they had any problems? If so, what?*

- *How are they organized?*

- *What can you tell me about the _____ department?*

- *Are you aware of any recent articles published about this organization or Websites—other than their own—that have information on them?*

- *Do you know anyone who might be able to give me more information about this organization?*

This kind of information from people with firsthand experience is a great complement to the information you get on the Internet. If you are a candidate for an executive job, especially at the C level (CEO, COO, CFO, and the like), these conversations about specific organizations are particularly important. Inside (though not proprietary, of course) information on the organization's people, plans, needs, and problems, combined with publicly available information, will enable you to make much better decisions about which organizations to concentrate on. In addition, this same information will be very useful in generating and evaluating offers.

Let's take a look at what you might say to get started with your Inner and Middle Circle personal contacts. The following is a sample script on that topic. Of course no one will do it exactly like this, but I hope it will give you some ideas you can use. The basic principles are very simple. Tell the truth. Make your networking partner comfortable. Guide the discussion and politely ask for what you want.

Script: Getting Started With an Inner or Middle Circle Personal Contact

You: Thanks for helping me with my job search. I really appreciate it. I don't always enjoy job hunting, and it sure is good to have somebody to talk to about it.

Them: No problem. What's a friend for? You'd do the same for me.

You: I want to start by explaining how I'm doing my job hunting. Would that be okay?

Them: Sure. That's great; go ahead.

You: I read a couple of job-hunting books by a guy named Orville Pierson. He's got 30 years experience helping people find jobs, and I think what he says makes sense. It's all about going after the right organizations before they have a job opening. The idea is that you talk to people at a number of potential employers. You get acquainted and let them know you're interested. And then when a job opening happens at one of them, you're in the right place at the right time.

Them: That sounds like a lot of work. Why don't you just use the Internet?

You: I'm doing that, too. And I'm checking the newspapers and using recruiters and sending out resumes. You're right, it's all a lot of work. But I guess I'm finding out that job hunting takes some work if you want to do it right. So far, I haven't gotten any interviews from the Internet and recruiters.

But I like what this guy Orville says. It's about being proactive. You don't wait for the opening. You go after the employers you like and when the opening happens, you're first in line. They already know you. I think it gives you a better chance of ending up at a place you really like because you get to know a whole bunch of places and then you put more work into the best ones.

Them: Is that what they call the hidden job market? The unadvertised jobs?

You: Yes, that's right. Anyway, I decided that what I want to do is _____ . I think that makes sense because of my experience in _____ , _____ , and _____ . Do you think that's the right direction for me?

Them: Yes. You've always liked that kind of work. It's a logical next step.

You: That's what I thought too. So what I did next was make up a list of organizations where I might want to work. Orville calls it a Target List. He says it's as important as a resume. That makes sense to me. I've decided to be really choosy. I don't want to work just any place. I want a place that I really like.

So I researched my list on the Internet. But you know how it is. The Internet doesn't tell you everything. I want to find out everything I can about these employers. Would you be willing to take a look at the list and see if you know anything about any of them?

Them: Sure.

While they're looking at the list, discuss all of the organizations they're familiar with and use the questions on page 145.

Get Introductions to New Personal and Professional Contacts

With your Inner Circle, always request and discuss introductions.
With Middle Circle contacts, be more cautious—but *do* ask.
With the Outer Circle contacts, introductions are less likely unless you have an organizational connection.

You don't want to be pushy about this, but it's always smart to ask your networking partners about other people you might talk to. As you noticed in the two previous question lists, there is a natural flow in the conversation. You and your partner discuss organizations. You ask questions about those organizations. When your partner doesn't know the answer to some of the questions, it's perfectly natural to ask if they might know someone who does have that information.

There is another way that it works too. When your networking partner gives you great information on a particular organization, always ask, *"How do you happen to know that?"* The answer is usually one of two things. Perhaps they read it or saw it on the Internet. If so, ask where they saw it so you can check it out.

Or, if you're lucky, it gets even better. They might have gotten information through people. They may have worked there themselves, or they might know someone who works there or know a former employee or a person with contact with the organization. Your networking partners won't always volunteer this information because they don't always know how important it is, so it's smart to ask.

Whenever any networking partner mentions the name of a person who might be a good future networking partner, you have two decisions to make: Will you ask for an introduction? And if so, when?

The rule of thumb with your Inner Circle is that you should always ask for an introduction. Or at least, you should always discuss that possibility. The question, as always, is whether your networking partner believes that you and this new person would be likely to get along—and whether your networking partner would be comfortable making the introduction. If the answer to both questions is yes, then you should certainly proceed.

With your Middle Circle contacts, be a little more cautious about asking for introductions. Many of your Middle Circle contacts will be happy to make introductions, but you shouldn't assume that they will. Ask. But ask more carefully and pay attention to their comfort level.

If you are going to ask for an introduction, your second decision is when to ask. Sometimes it's better to jot down the names as they are mentioned during the conversation and then inquire at the end of the conversation about introductions. If, for example, eight names are mentioned, you might select only the four that seem the most important and ask for only four introductions—saving the rest for later after you've talked to the first four.

With a good friend in your Inner Circle, you might discuss the matter with them and get their opinion on which of the eight you should talk to and when. The two of you may decide that you should talk to all of them, or none.

When your networking partner is willing to make an introduction, there are several ways that can be done. One way is for your networking partner to set up a meeting—a lunch perhaps—with the three of you. This is usually an easy and comfortable way for you to get acquainted with the new person. You may want to volunteer in advance to pay for such a lunch.

Another highly effective choice is for your networking partner to telephone the new person, tell them about you, and ask if they'd be willing to talk to you. Friends in your Inner Circle might be more than happy to do this. This step makes your first conversation with the new person much easier because your networking partner does some of the initial explaining for you. The new person is then not only expecting your call, but possibly even looking forward to it. Let's take a look at how this part might work in another suggested script.

Script: Asking For Introductions From Inner and Middle Circle Personal Contacts

You: While we were talking about my Target List, you mentioned six different people. Four of them are people who are working inside of employers on the list. Two are people you said might have more information.

Them: You wrote their names down? You're really serious about this, aren't you?

You: Yes. I'm doing things like I do them at work. I'm writing things down. Making lists. Checking things off and getting them done. I'm not looking for just any job. I'm planning to get a really good one.

Them: Well that's good, but I don't see how those six people are going to help you. They're not high enough. They're just people like us.

You: People like us are exactly who I want to talk to right now. You said four of the six are working inside companies on my list. Those four can give me the lowdown on four different companies—inside stuff. And if they wanted to, they could introduce me to the Decision Maker, the person who could hire me, my next boss. Right now, whether there's an opening or not.

But the important question right now is whether you think it would be a good idea for me to talk to them. And whether you would be comfortable introducing me to them.

Them: Now I get it. I see what you're doing. This is smart.

You: I'd really like to have your opinion on whether it would be a good idea for me to talk to those four. I only want to talk to your friends if you think it's going to work out. I certainly don't want to cause any problems for you.

Them: Well, those four aren't exactly my friends. They're just people I know. And I do think you should talk to three of them.

You: Good. Can we talk about those three?

Them: Don't you want to know why I'm keeping you away from Mike?

You: Sure, if you want to tell me.

Them: It's no big secret. He's a jerk. A complete idiot. But he does work at one of your companies.

You: If there's a lot of jerks over there, I'm going to take it off my list.

Them: He's the only one I know of. But the other three are all good people. Two of them I really like, and the third one's okay.

You: Would you be willing to call them and introduce me? Let them know that I'll be giving them a call? Would you be comfortable doing that?

Them: Sure, I could do that with two of them. But the third one, I don't know so well. What if I sent her an e-mail?

You: Two phone calls and an e-mail would be just great. I would really appreciate it.

Them: No problem. I'm happy to talk to those two anyway. And you know, I'd be happy to call those other two as well, the ones who don't work in any of your companies. Those two are both good friends of mine. I talk to them all the time. One, Jim, is a guy you will really like. I've been wanting you to meet him.

You: That's great. Thank you. And with Jim, how would you feel about my taking the two of you out to lunch sometime? He and I could get acquainted. I promise I wouldn't talk about job hunting the whole time.

Them: And you're buying?

You: Absolutely. Sandwiches. Really good sandwiches, at a really nice place. One that doesn't have white tablecloths, because I'm unemployed right now.

Them: It's a deal. You'll like him.

In the e-mail alternative, your networking partner tells the new person why they think the two of you would enjoy meeting. They also mention that you're in a job search and looking for information. *"I think you would enjoy meeting Pat because..."* is usually a good line to include, and the two of you can discuss what the reasons are. When the new person responds by e-mail, your networking partner can forward the e-mail to you and let you know that it's time for you to make the phone call.

Please notice that I'm suggesting phone calls. Networking is possible in a series of back-and-forth e-mails, but it's usually much more effective in a real-time conversation. This is especially true when you are first meeting a new person. In fact, with a new person, an in-person meeting is the best of all. It gives you a better chance to get acquainted and the talk is more likely to last longer. Such a meeting can be "coffee," lunch, or whatever you're both comfortable with. In some cases of personal contacts, it might even be at your house or theirs.

The third choice on introductions—Do-It-Yourself—is not as good as the first two, but it does work. You can ask your networking partner for permission to use their name in introducing yourself to the new person. There are two drawbacks with going this way. The first is that this approach has been abused in networking. Believe it or not, some job-search networkers use people's names without permission and sometimes even use the names of people they've never met. Personally, I think both of those are very bad moves.

The other drawback is simply that your job is a bit more difficult when introducing yourself. People are less likely to take your call, so you may need to be more persistent. You might also have to work a little harder when you do get on the phone, because the new contact has no information on you—and could even be a little suspicious at first.

I hope that your Inner Circle friends will be willing to make telephone, e-mail, or personal introductions for you. Sometimes people in your Middle Circle will do that as well. But using your networking partner's name does work just fine when it's done with permission—and sometimes it's the better choice with Middle Circle contacts.

When you do that, sometimes it's smart to first send an e-mail mentioning your networking partner's name in the subject line (so the new contact knows it's not spam), introducing yourself in the e-mail and telling them when you will call them. This tells the new person that they can expect a call, and it also gives them the opportunity to check with the person who made the introduction before they talk to you if they want to.

We've been talking about asking for the most obvious introductions—to people with a known connection to your targets or to information you need. I think it's also smart to ask for—and be receptive to—introductions to other new people, even when there is no obvious reason.

We know from Professor Watts and his "clusters" that this kind of introduction can sometimes catapult you into a new network in which you had no prior connections at all. You can open this door simply by asking, *Is there anyone else that you think I should meet—perhaps someone with no obvious connection to my Target List?"*

One last thing about introductions: Be sure to follow up promptly after the introduction is made. It's the polite thing to do and it's also more effective.

NETWORKING WITH YOUR OUTER CIRCLE OF PERSONAL CONTACTS

Most of what we've said also applies to networking with your Outer Circle of personal contacts. But you probably cannot go as far with this group as quickly as you can with your Inner and Middle Circles.

With some, you may decide to stop after getting your message out. Remember, when you do that effectively, you've taken an important and useful step in job hunting. It's perfectly okay to stop there.

Or you may decide to simply mention a limited number of your targets in conversation rather than showing them the whole list. Check to see if they know anything about that smaller verbal list. If so, you can have a conversation similar to those where you use your list. It won't be as thorough, but it will be less formal and more social. And it could be just as effective.

Another possibility is e-mailing your Target List—with their permission, of course—after the first telephone conversation instead of before it. Then you would make a second call to see what comments they might have.

With people who don't know you well—or at all—asking for introductions to others may be going too far. Although you need to make your own judgments based on how the conversation goes and how strong the connection feels to both of you, I'd certainly suggest caution. If you handle it well, you might ask for—and get—introductions from a quarter of your Outer Circle contacts, compared to nearly all of your Inner Circle contacts.

Outer Circle contacts where you have a strong organizational connection—religious, fraternal/sororal, or alumni, for example—are an exception to this rule of thumb. In these passive or dormant categories, you will get a much higher percentage of people willing to make introductions, even when they don't know you well.

If the contacts are dormant—people you haven't talked to for a long time—you certainly need to start by catching up on what's happened in the intervening months or years. After that, it may be appropriate to continue with your job-search agenda—or not. You can get your 30-second Core Message into the conversation with just about anyone, because it's about what's happening in your life right now—as in, "what's up?"—and a logical part of the conversation.

Once you open up the topic of your job hunting, see how they respond. Then decide if you'll go farther. If you decide not to, have a nice talk with them anyway. Hey, it's okay to have some fun now and then, even if you're job hunting. Maybe you'll decide to raise the topic of job hunting in a later conversation. Maybe you won't.

With passive networking connections, you should probably look for those where you have double or triple shared-interest connections. If one of the shared interests is that they are currently employed at one of your targeted organizations, you should probably treat the call more as a professional contact networking call (see Chapter Eight), and get right down to business.

THE OUTER CIRCLE AND COLD CALLS

I think it's important to talk about the fuzzy boundary between talking to Outer Circle contacts and making cold calls. "Cold call" is a sales term that refers to talking to total strangers, people who have never heard of you, people with whom you have no connection whatsoever.

For example, a salesperson selling coffee or office supplies might go into a large office building and visit each and every organization in the building, trying to strike up conversations and sell a product. A telemarketer might take out the phone book and starting with the A's, call everyone in the book, making a sales pitch to each. (Or at least they might have done that before it became illegal with the do-not-call laws.) Both of these examples are cold calls.

Some job-hunting books recommend cold calling as a job-hunting method and some even confuse it with networking. I'm not surprised by the confusion, because the dividing line between networking in your Outer Circle and cold calling is anything but clear.

Personally, I would almost never recommend the walk-in version of cold calling for professional-level job hunters. The telephone cold-calling version does work in job hunting—if you can tolerate it. Some sales-oriented people are completely comfortable with calling total strangers and good at involving them in conversations. These rare people are also okay with the fact that the majority of such calls go nowhere, because a small percentage turn out to be productive.

It looks to me like fewer than one percent of job hunters are comfortable and effective with cold calling. But if you're one of those and are happy making the hundreds of calls that it will take, I recommend it. For everyone else, cold calling is a last resort. It might be a good idea to try some cold calls now and then, when you can't find a better way to get inside a target. But doing it all the time is difficult for most of us.

Many people who are good at cold calling are effective because they look for—and sometimes find—some common interests with the stranger they called. In other words, the closer the call gets to being networking, the easier it is.

I usually recommend starting with your strongest connections and moving gradually out toward cold calls. In reaching out through your Inner, then Middle, then Outer Circles in networking, you are talking to people with whom you have less and less connection. When working in your Outer Circle, you will sooner or later cross the line into cold calling. As you get closer to that dividing line, a higher percentage of your calls will be unproductive.

Sometimes people call networking contacts "warm calls" to contrast them with the cold calling sales technique. I think the name is accurate, because in your Inner Circle, you'll usually get a warm welcome. In your Middle Circle, the welcome is also usually warm, or at least polite. When you cross over into cold calling, warmth and welcomes are no longer a given. You have to work harder.

GATHER YOUR COURAGE AND WORK THE COOL ZONE

A common mistake in job-search networking is to work only with the easiest Inner Circle contacts and stop there. An effective job hunter involves the vast majority of their Inner Circle contacts and thoroughly works with Middle Circle contacts.

You may also need to push well into the Outer Circle, and even into the cool zone at its outer edge. This takes more courage, because it's likely that you'll have some calls that turn out to be ice cold, rather than merely cool. These experiences can be discouraging.

But if you don't make the effort, you might miss some career opportunities, and some great experiences connecting or re-connecting with some great people.

Don't do it right away. Start with Inner, then move to Middle. As you do that, your Inner and Middle Circle contacts will introduce you to new ones. You'll work with the new ones and continue to work with the original contacts.

But after you've gotten your search moving and you have some networking experience under your belt, move into the Outer Circle, and press on into the cool zone. With a little experience you'll figure out where the line is for you. But be courageous. Push the envelope a bit. You might end up connecting with just the right person.

Because you're never sure how things will go with Outer Circle personal contacts, I'm going to give you two different scripts for talking to a dormant contact: worst- and best-case scenarios. Let's start with the worst, and get it out of the way.

Script: Getting Started With a Dormant Outer Circle Personal Contact—Worst Case

You: This is Pat Person calling. May I speak to Bill Nichols?

Them: This is Bill.

You: Bill, I don't know if you remember, but you and I were classmates at State University. We used to sit next to each other in Bio.

Bill: We did?

You: Yes, and we were also in the same English Lit class. We did a Hemingway project together.

Bill: What did you say your name was?

You: Pat. Pat Person.

Bill: I'm sorry, I don't remember. That was a long time ago. Is this about the Alumni Fund? I'm never made a donation and I'm not going to start now.

You: No, it's not about the Alumni Fund. I've been reconnecting with some people from State. I remembered you and thought I'd give you a call.

Bill: How did you get my number? It's unlisted.

You: I found you online. It sounds like this isn't a good time for you.

Bill: No, it's not.

You: I'm sorry I bothered you. Good-bye.

This kind of Outer Circle networking call is like one of those old TV quiz shows. The host asks you to pick one of the three curtains for your prize. One of the prizes is a scruffy old goat chained to a post. But behind another curtain is a brand new luxury car, all taxes paid, just drive it home. Lets take a look at that possibility.

Script: Getting Started With a Dormant Outer Circle Personal Contact—Best Case

You: This is Pat Person calling. May I speak to Bill Nichols?

Them: PAT!! PAT PERSON!! I've was just thinking about you the other day! How are you?

You: Great. And you?

Them: Fabulous. I can't believe it's you. How long has it been? Do your remember bio at State? Professor Froggy? And Schultz in the front row? And the Hemingway project?

With this one, there's going to be a lot of catching up. Sooner or later, the conversation is going to get to what you're doing now. Then you can honestly tell them about your job search, your networking, and how you're using job search as an excuse to catch up with people you haven't talked to for years. And how you've got time to do that because you're unemployed. And how much fun you're having, at least sometimes.

Then you will decide whether to go more deeply into the job-hunting conversation now or to do it in a subsequent call, maybe after you e-mail your Target List.

Of course, most Outer Circle calls will be somewhere between these two extremes. With some, you may decide not to bring up your job hunting at all. With others, you may get numerous referrals and information on where to find other dormant Outer Circle contacts, people you've lost touch with. Information on your Target List is a good possibility, as are all the other things we discussed in this chapter. Once you get past the catching up, many conversations will be much like your Inner and Middle Circle conversations.

Passive contacts in your Outer Circle are one step closer to cold calls, and sometimes more like a professional contact. With a call to a fellow university alum that you'd never met, you'd probably want a double or triple common interest. One excellent possibility is that your Internet research shows that person working inside one of your target companies, or living in a city or country that's part of your Target Market.

If you select a person because of where they work, the conversation would likely be limited to that organization only, and you would be pursuing that organization more than doing general networking. You would treat it more like a professional contact. This is another example of effective networking in the cool zone.

Getting Started With People You Just Met

However you are introduced to new people, you should contact them soon after the introduction. Ideally, you arrange with the original personal contact exactly how and when you'll talk to the new one.

The number-one common interest with these new contacts is usually the person who introduced you, and that's a good place to start the conversation. If your original contact gave you more information about the new one, you can and should refer to that in the call.

Here's an example of how it might go.

Script: Getting Started With a New Personal Contact After an Introduction

You: This is Pat Person calling. I'm a friend of Jane Frick. Did she call you about me?

Them: Yes, she did. She really said some nice things about you.

You: Well, that was kind of her. She and I have known each other for years and I have a high opinion of her too. She's a lovely person. How do you happen to know her?

Them: She and I have done volunteer work together for years at...

(This conversation about Jane and any other shared interests may go on for a while. We'll skip to the end of it.)

You: Did Jane happen to mention that I'm job hunting right now?

Them: Yes, and she said that I didn't have to know any senior executives in order to be helpful. Which is a good thing, because I only met one in my life and I can't remember his name.

You: Well, she's right. You don't have to know any executives and I appreciate your willingness to help out. I'd like to start by telling you a little bit about what I'm doing. Would that be okay?

Them: Yes.

You: The kind of work I'm looking for is _____ . I think that makes sense because of my experience in _____, _____, and _____ . But just as important, I really enjoy that kind of work. I've been doing it for the last seven years and I'd still be at it if there hadn't been a big downsizing.

I'm listed on the Internet job boards. I'm also following the ads and postings, and I'm registered with staffing agencies.

Them: It sounds like you're really doing a full-scale job search.

You: Yes, I've read some books on it and I'm pulling out all the stops. But I actually think the most important part is talking to people like you to see if I can get information on the employers I'm most interested in.

Them: I'd be glad to help if I can, but I don't know much about employers except for the hospital where I work. And they're only hiring nurses right now—certainly nothing like the jobs you're looking for.

You: I don't expect you to know about job openings. I'm working on that part on the Internet. What I'm hoping you might be able to help with is information on organizations. I've made a list of about 40 organizations where I think I'd like to work. About half are in healthcare. I don't know if any of them have openings right now, but sooner or later one of them will.

Them: Forty! Wow, that's a lot.

You: Yes, it is a lot, but the bigger the list is, the more likely that one will have an opening soon. I want to get acquainted with them before they have the opening.

Right now, I'm working on finding out more about them: What they do, how well they're doing, how they treat their employees—that kind of thing. I wonder if you'd be willing to look at my list and see if you know anything about any of them. Or maybe if you know someone who might know. Or someone who works at one of them. Would you be willing to do that?

Them: Sure. I can't promise that I'll know anything about them, but I'm happy to take a look.

You: That's great. May I e-mail you the list and call back to see if you recognize any of them?

Them: Sure. That's fine.

You: When would be a good time for me to call back?

If possible, of course, you'd e-mail the list while you're both still on the phone.

You might decide to set up an in-person meeting. You could do this at the very beginning of the call right after you introduce yourself. Or you could do it at the end, instead of e-mailing the list and setting up a second phone call. Sometimes it's good to ask the advice of the person introducing you on which would be better.

Notice that you're not giving them a resume yet. You should definitely do that after discussing the list, and you might decide to do it sooner—if it won't distract the conversation from the list.

Playful Personal Networking

Sometimes the best way to find a job is to forget about finding a job.

Just talk with people.

We started this discussion by talking about goals in job-search networking. I will say again that I think being clear on your goals is very important. But, at the same time, I think it's good to see networking as a game or a journey—something more playful than a job hunt.

You don't know what will happen along the way. Even though it's not your goal in job hunting, you might make some new friends. Although you are looking for information, and sometimes help, you might also be *providing* information and help—in addition to getting it or even instead of getting it.

Sometimes job hunters find real satisfaction in the opportunity to help others along the way. Sometimes this help is something very simple, such as providing information on effective job hunting. These days, most people are aware that they are likely to change jobs repeatedly through the course of their careers. Your taking the time to tell them what you've learned about that could be a real service for them.

Sometimes, you discover your networking partner's interests in your conversations with them. If you record and remember those interests, you may later be able to offer to introduce them to people they might enjoy meeting. Or send them an e-mail with a link to a Website that relates to that interest.

You don't know what might happen along the way in networking. You might have interesting conversations that have nothing to do with job hunting. You might learn all kinds of new things. You might just plain have fun.

During the course of my career, I have often had conversations with job hunters who have landed jobs by networking. They frequently tell me that looking back through the course of their job-• search networking, they see any number of other benefits in addition to a great new job. Sometimes—no kidding!—people actually tell me that a period of unemployment combined with job-search networking was a great blessing.

So after you carefully plan your networking, I'd like to suggest that you forget about the planning. Just get started talking to people and see where it leads.

Always Give Them Your Resume—Afterward

Many job hunters give their networking partners their resumes right away, at the beginning of a meeting or conversation. Or they e-mail it before they call.

What usually happens next is a discussion of the resume and how it can be improved, and a discussion of who to send the resume to, or who to give it to in person. Although all of these can be useful conversations, they're most useful when done in the right way at the right time with the right person.

The best person to help you improve your resume is someone who is a current or former Decision Maker in your field. Second best is someone who knows those people well because they worked with them in one way or another. This could be a recruiter, a career coach, the Decision Maker's boss, or someone who has worked for a Decision Maker of that kind. Once you have the content you need, an experienced resume writer might help you say it better and a proofreader is essential. Asking people other than these for resume help could be a waste of time.

The other problem with giving people your resume is that they often focus on resume distribution, rather than networking. There's nothing wrong with resume distribution. You should do it. But don't let it be a substitute for networking.

It's great when someone offers to pass your resume along to someone they know, and you should certainly accept that offer—if it's the only thing they're comfortable doing. However, it would be much better for your job search if they'd be comfortable introducing you to those other people and letting you give them the resume yourself. After you've talked to them.

Moving to New Contacts, Personal and Professional

Your initial personal contacts should result in introductions to new contacts. Not everyone will be comfortable making them, but if you're not getting introductions from at least half of your Inner Circle personal contacts, you probably aren't asking. Or you may not be explaining what you're doing well enough to make people comfortable.

If this happens to you, it might be smart to talk it over with your confidantes or your coach. Your experience with your Inner Circle is where you learn how to play this networking game. Don't move to your Middle and Outer Circles until you've learned what you need to learn and feel ready.

Your initial contacts could introduce you to more personal contacts or to professional contacts. If they have professional introductions for you, be sure you're well prepared before you make those contacts. If, for example, your very first Inner Circle contact is able to introduce you to a high level professional contact, a Decision Maker, you might want to discuss postponing that important introduction until you had all the information you needed to make a good impression.

Of course, moving to professional contacts is one of the goals of talking to personal contacts. You certainly want to get to them as soon as you can. The next chapter is on networking with those professional contacts—the other central part of the "Talk" section of the Decide-Prepare-Talk-Land sequence we discussed in Chapter Two.

ORVILLE'S JOURNAL

Orville and Ben Become Co-Authors

"So he starts screaming. No kidding. Yelling. I had the phone two feet from my ear and it was still too loud." Ben was back in my office, filling me in on a networking call. "'You're an idiot!' he says. 'You're a friend of Fred's? You're a complete sleazeball.'"

"Fred introduced the two of you?"

"Not exactly. I got the guy's name off of Fred's Web page."

"A social networking site?"

"Yeah. But I never talked to Fred. I found the guy's phone number and called him."

"Oops."

"Yeah, no kidding. Job-hunting lesson #37: Always talk to Fred. They had a business deal that went bad."

"What happened in the rest of your networking last week?" I figured it was time to get past that one and do my coaching job. "How many contacts did you make and what kind?"

Ben set his tea down. I finally had him hooked on Jasmine green. He liked the Dragon Pearl, with a little sugar.

"I had six great conversations. Lots of good information and two introductions to Decision Makers. I'm going to call those two next week. I'm ready for them."

"Good."

"Another 18 calls that were okay. I got some information and some introductions."

"Eighteen more? Great."

"And four that went nowhere. Plus Fred's former friend."

"Twenty-nine total?"

"Yes, and a lot of Internet research. I'm researching my targets."

"It sounds like you're completely back on track."

"Yes, and I've got a couple in the cool zone that I'm going to try next week. Along with at least a dozen more Inner and Middle Circle people. And I'm visiting with Rachel. We have an hour scheduled."

"A serious meeting with Rachel? Great. But why the cool zone moves?"

"I thought of a couple of people that might have good information. They're inside of possible targets. I don't have a strong connection to them. It's passive. But I figured I'd try." He paused. "And I'm going to call Miles, the Super Bowl guy."

"Why not?" I smiled. "If Fred's former friend didn't stop you, I can't see how cool calls would."

Ben got out of the rocker and moved to the chair next to my desk. "Now we're going to talk about your networking book."

"My book? You finally read it?"

"Yes. You've been helping me with my search. I'm going to help you with the book. It's very good. But there's something you left out. Voice mail."

"Ah, voice mail. The bane of job hunters. I hate it."

"But you've got to put it in the book."

"Why? With personal contacts, it's not a problem. With professional contacts, I want people to avoid it. If you get voice mail, hang up. Call back later. Try early or late."

"But you know that doesn't always work."

"Yes, you're right. So tell me the solution."

"You leave a voice mail with the name of the person who introduced you. So-and so-suggested I call."

"And not tell them what it's about? At work, everyone wants to know why you're calling."

"Well, you can mention some common interest. Tell them you have something for them. Some useful information."

"And not mention job search? Then later, when they find out you're job hunting, won't they feel like it's bait and switch?"

"Well, maybe. But maybe not. You could leave the whole thing on the voice mail. What you're doing in search and why. Explain it."

"That's possible. A little long, but possible."

"So that's four possible voice-mail solutions. But we both know that the fifth one is the best, right?"

"Tell me."

"You get the person making the introduction to call or e-mail the new person before you do. Then the voice mail with the name of the person referring you will probably do it. And all of the other solutions do work. At least sometimes."

"You're right. The fifth solution is the best by far."

"So put it in," Ben said. He was standing up, heading for the door.

"Okay." I said, "It's in. You want your name on the cover above or below mine?"

"Below. Pierson, Williams. Alphabetical."

He left. I went back to my writing.

Your Professional Networks

LEVEL THREE	Work-related contacts not in targeted organizations.
LEVEL TWO	Professional peers and Insiders at your targets.
LEVEL ONE	Decision Makers and Influencers inside your targets.
DECIDE	PREPARE	**TALK**	LAND

Chapter Eight

Build Your Professional Networks

Effective networking, as we said back in Chapter Two, is about deciding to do it well, preparing to network, talking to the right people in the right way, getting through to the Decision Maker, and landing a job. Of course, talking to people is the heart of the process.

In the previous chapter, we looked at talking to personal contacts and how that's a great way to get your job search moving. In fact, I've seen many, many job hunters who never get much beyond personal contacts. They talk to friends and acquaintances and someone happens to know someone at the right organization. They make a phone call, get an interview, and it's done—without any professional networking at all.

This could happen to you. But if you're reading this chapter, it probably hasn't happened yet, and you maybe shouldn't plan on it. So keep on doing your personal networking, but when you're ready, move on to professional contacts as well. Most job hunters use a combination of personal and professional contacts.

By professional contacts, I mean people you work with, have worked with in the past, or might work with in the future. Please note that this group is a network. Or several networks. Members of these networks share an interest in a particular kind of work or a particular kind of organization. When you're employed, you discuss these shared professional and organizational interests all the time.

If you happen to meet someone at a party who is in an occupation similar to yours, that kind of work is a possible conversation topic. You might compare notes. You might both learn something that makes you more effective at work. You sometimes find that the two of you know some of the same people. So the kind of professional networking we're talking about can happen without your planning it.

In this chapter, we're going to look at using professional networking in a planned and highly effective way in your job search. Let's start with the easiest part: professional contacts who are also friends.

If some of your professional contacts are also personal contacts, you are truly blessed in your job-search efforts. The double shared interest makes it even more likely that they'll be able to help you and be interested in doing so. This kind of conversations is usually easy and comfortable. If you have contacts like this, I'd suggest putting them high on your list and contacting them early.

On the other hand, if you're a recent graduate who hasn't done any internships or summer jobs, you may not have any professional contacts at all. Your job-search networking will be the beginning of building a professional network. Most job hunters expand their professional networks during a search. You'll need to do that more than most and will probably have to work a little harder on this part. But like everyone else, you will certainly find opportunities to be introduced to professional contacts by personal contacts.

Treat Professional Contacts Differently From Personal

Be more cautious about asking for favors.

Offer information as well as asking for it.

Don't use your Target List with Insiders.

Be judicious about asking for referrals.

All job hunters should be talking to both personal and professional contacts. It's important to think of those two groups separately and to treat them differently. Sometimes job hunters make the mistake of thinking that "networking is networking," and it makes no difference to whom you're talking. Then they talk to professional contacts as if they were friends and wonder why it doesn't work so well.

The most important difference is usually asking for favors, even small ones. When you're talking to an Inner or Middle Circle personal contact, you're in a world where people routinely help each other in many ways. The person you're talking to might be a fellow community member as well as a networking partner. In many communities, taking five or 10 minutes or even an hour to have a chat or look at a Target List is just part of what people do. In a community of friends, people may not even see it as doing favors. It's just the way it is.

But with people who are professional contacts and nothing more, you need to think more carefully about what you're asking someone to do. You will probably find some professional contacts who will go out of their way to assist you. Some will have a motive for doing that—such as wanting to look good to their employer by bringing in a great job candidate, for example. Or hoping that later on, when you're in a new executive position, you'll help them out in some way. Others will simply do it without expecting any benefit for themselves.

You will also find professional contacts who have no interest at all in assisting you. But these same people may nonetheless be very interested in talking to you as a professional networking partner—if you know how to be a good one and behave that way. If you're doing your job in collecting relevant information, you'll be interesting to talk to. Your networking partners will value you as an information source that helps them do their job better and advance their careers. They will be willing to take some time out of their work day to talk to you, or to do that before or after work.

Another change from personal to professional contacts is the use of your Target List. You know by now that I strongly recommend using that list or some of its contents with most of your personal contacts. With your professional contacts, there are situations where you should use it in exactly the same way. But, as you'll see in this chapter, there are other situations where it would be a mistake even to mention that you have a Target List.

The same is true of referrals. With professional contacts, you'll need to be more judicious about who you ask to introduce you to others. Mostly it's appropriate and a really good idea. But in some situations, it could make a bad impression on someone who is just getting acquainted with you.

Finally, there's a difference in how you talk to people. With professional contacts, you usually need to be more formal and business-like. It's about getting things done and it's sometimes an opportunity to show people how effective you can be in focused, work-oriented conversations. It's about useful information. It's less social than networking with personal contacts.

The ultimate professional contact, of course, is the Decision Maker, the person who could be your next boss. With that person, your conversation might be friendly, but it should be all business and certainly not about wasting their time. This conversation is always a job interview. Or at least that's how you should treat it, regardless of how the Decision Maker sees it.

Working Your Way Up the Ladder of Professional Contacts

Start with Level Three, work-related contacts not in targeted organizations. Then move to Level Two, professional peers and Insiders at your targets. Then to Level One, Decision Makers and Influencers inside your targets.

Of course, you probably won't start with the Decision Maker. You'll probably work your way up to that. There's a continuum of professional contacts. You can picture it as a ladder: at the bottom end of it are the professional contacts who are also Inner Circle personal contacts, community members, and maybe good friends. At the top end are the Decision Makers you never met, people you are considering for the job of being your next boss.

At the lower end of that ladder, you're behaving in the same way you did with your personal contacts. Your job is to work your way to the top, where the Decision Makers are. The closer you get to the top, the more you are behaving in a strictly professional manner—just as you might if you already worked there.

You are working your way, step by step up the ladder and into the right job in the right organization. You are always looking for ways to get introduced to people higher on the ladder by someone you already know.

In looking at how to best manage your conversations within this continuum of contacts, it helps to divide them into three groups, even though the boundaries between the groups are sometimes fuzzy. I'm going to use this device, calling them Levels Three, Two, and One. Level Three is at the bottom, and you're working your way up to Level One, where your next job is. This is summarized in the chart on page 176.

All three levels are professional contacts, connections relating to work. Twos and Ones do work similar to the work you do or work in organizations on your Target List. You probably know more Threes than Ones.

Level Three includes professional contacts who are not in the same line of work as you are. They do not currently work inside of any of your targeted organizations. Some work in jobs in which they have regular contact with people in your profession or your targeted organizations. Some do not.

Level Two includes people you know who work inside your targets, below your level or in departments you're not interested in. This level also includes your peers, people in jobs similar to the job you want. These professional peers may or may not work inside a targeted organization.

The Ladder of Networking Contacts

Start at the bottom and work your way up

Whenever you use your Target List, look for the opportunity to get introduced to new people

Professional Contacts

Level One	**Decision Makers and Influencers**	Do not use your Target List
Level Two	**Insiders and professional peers**	Use your Target List with professional peers, but not with Insiders
Level Three	**All other work related contacts**	Use your Target List or mention some targets

Personal Contacts

Outer Circle Including the cool zone	**Dormant contacts:** former Inner or Middle, but no recent contact **Passive contacts:** you have an organizational or community connection, but never met this particular person	When appropriate, use your Target List or mention some targets
Middle Circle	**Community and organizational contacts** that you have met	Use your Target List or mention some targets
Inner Circle	**Friends, acquaintances, and relatives**, people you talk to regularly	Always use your Target List

You are talking to professional peers because they have information on your profession or your targeted organizations. Because they do the same kind of work as you, they may have worked at one of your targets in the past, and they may know people currently inside your targets.

Then there's Level One. This is where you're going, your goal. Your number one Level One contact, of course, is the Decision Maker who could be your next boss. Also included in Level One is your boss's boss and anyone higher than that.

This level also includes Influencers. These are people who have your next boss's ear, people your Decision Maker trusts. Very often people who report to the Decision Maker are Level One Influencers. But some of the Decision Maker's direct reports might only be Level Two Insiders, people with little influence, but still very useful information sources. And there may also be people who are highly influential with the Decision Maker, but who do not report to that person.

Getting your message to this Level One group is a key goal of your search. Meeting them—even for a few minutes standing in a hallway—is a big advantage.

You may need to meet only one Decision Maker before getting hired. Sometimes it happens that way. But it's more likely to take a dozen or two. What is certain is this: The more Level One contacts you make, the closer you are to a new job. So you're always keeping an eye out for them.

It's entirely possible to jump from a personal friend straight to a Decision Maker. When you have the opportunity to do that, make sure you're prepared before accepting the introduction. If there's any doubt that you're ready, delay making the contact until you are fully prepared. This kind of leap can accelerate your search dramatically. Sometimes—whoosh!—it takes you straight into an interview and offer.

But more often, you'll need to work your way up from personal contacts to Level Three professional contacts then Two, then One.

Let's take a more detailed look at all three levels, and discuss how to best handle each and how to move from one level to another as effective job hunters usually do in a well-planned search.

Level Three Professional Contacts

Include dormant and passive contacts as well as active.

These people are a great information source.

Look for those who know your targets.

Use your Target List or mention targets.

Level Three contacts include a wide range of people you have met in the workplace. The point is that you're already connected to them, so it's not difficult to get the chance to talk to them. Some of these may also be personal friends or close associates. At the other extreme, like Outer Circle personal contacts, some of these are dormant or passive.

Because they're in the workplace, your Level Three contacts are well positioned to assist you in attaining your networking goals. Level Threes can always help you attain the goal of collecting information that will help you decide exactly what jobs and organizations to pursue. They can also provide information that will make you more effective in pursuing those organizations. Level Three professional contacts are more likely than personal contacts to understand the workplace issues you're contemplating and have the information you need.

If gathering information for decision-making is particularly important for you, you might be smart to stay with Level Three conversations for a while and not rush into Levels Two and One. In Level Three, you're talking with people not inside your targeted organizations. Sometimes it's good to stay with this until you've learned enough to make the right decisions and to present yourself well at the higher levels.

Another networking goal is getting the word out about your job search. This is easier to do with professional contacts because it's a work-related conversation, and some of them may know your work. Your Level Three contacts are in the workplace and may also know the people and organizations that you're interested in. So spreading the word here is easy, important, and very likely to be useful.

One thing to think about with Level Three contacts is: Who do they know? Who do they routinely talk to as part of their jobs? An executive looking for the right large business should consider consultants. There are consultants who regularly work with top managers at large businesses. They may want to do someone at a client organization a favor by introducing you. They have a great deal of information, some of which they could share with you if they wanted to. The same can be true of bankers or venture capitalists.

Interested in social service agencies? A psychologist or social worker might often refer clients to a wide range of them and know people at all of them.

Anyone—in business, not-for-profits, or government—should consider Threes who are salespeople. Is there a sales representative who sells something to your Level One or Two contacts? If so, that salesperson might introduce you as a favor to their customers, who could then get a look at a good job candidate without paying a fee.

Pharmaceutical and medical equipment reps, for example, talk to healthcare professionals all the time and may know healthcare organizations very well. Parts and equipment salespeople talk to manufacturers. The list is endless. Whether your targets are business, government, or not-for-profits, someone is selling them something.

And it's not just salespeople. Part of your job at Level Three is to look for people whose work has them talking to your targeted organizations and people, formally or informally. Sometimes the connections are obvious. Sometimes not. Talk to your Level Threes and find out.

Another networking goal is meeting Level Two and One contacts, Insiders at targeted organizations. Your personal contacts will introduce you to some of these. Your Level Three contacts can introduce you to more.

With most of your Level Three professional contacts, you should use your Target List. If they are also personal contacts, do it exactly as you would with Inner Circle personal contacts. It they are purely professional contacts, treat them like Middle or Outer Circle personal contacts. Be selective about using the list. You may want to do it verbally. In some cases, using the list won't be a good idea.

In talking to Threes, you can sometimes use the same language you use with personal contacts, so you may want to look again at the scripts in Chapter Seven.

Level Two Professional Contacts

Talk about your Target List with professional peers, but not with Insiders.

Gather information from Insiders about the organization, its needs and goals.

Find out what you can about the Decision Maker.

Level Two includes two kinds of contacts. First, there are professional peers, people in jobs like the one you want. They almost certainly have important information that you don't. Some are inside your targets, some are not.

Level Two also includes people you know who work inside any of your targeted organizations, but below your level or in departments you're not interested in joining. Insiders of any kind have useful information and can easily get your message to the right people.

If you make the right impression on them, many Level Twos will introduce you to Ones or to other Twos. If you don't know them well, or have just been introduced to them, you may have to work a bit harder to prepare to network effectively with them. You'll need to have topics of conversation that interest them.

If they're not Insiders, you might talk to professional peers about your targets or show them your Target List. With Insiders at your targets, it's usually better not to mention your Target List. Just talk about how interested you are in that particular organization.

If you're asking about other organizations as well, these Insiders could get the impression that your interest isn't really that strong. It's kind of like prospective boyfriends or girlfriends. If you're talking to one, it might not be smart to talk about too many of your other prospects. So it could a bad idea to show your Target List to Insiders, or even to reveal that you have one.

Because you want to convey your strong interest in joining the organization that you're talking to, any information you collect from Level Two Insiders should be limited to their organization. The more you know about your targets the better, and current Insiders are the very best source of information.

You shouldn't be asking for basic information. You should already have that. After all, how will anyone believe that you're interested if you haven't done any research? The better informed you are when you first show up, the better an impression you'll make.

There are two kinds of information to go after with Level Two Insiders. One kind is information for a final check on whether you want to work there. This is delicate. You will probably want to read between the lines more than asking direct questions, especially in examining possible negatives. But you should be doing a final check on whether this is the right place for you. If it's not, start treating these contacts as Level Threes.

The other kind of information you want is information that will help you get the job. Here, you can ask direct questions such as:

- *What are the expectations for that job title?*
- *What are they working on in that department right now?*
- *What skills are most needed?*
- *What are the main priorities?*

This kind of information will allow you to most effectively promote your candidacy and to interview well when you get to that point. Your questions should be based on what you found out in previous research on the Internet or by talking to outsiders familiar with the organization. Use discretion with this kind of inquiry. Some of this information could be seen as inappropriate to share with an outsider.

The primary focus of your questions is the organization's needs and goals. As you get this information, link your experience to those needs and goals. Let them know how you can help them. Don't hesitate to tell them how much you'd like to work there whenever the next opportunity arises.

"Who's who" information can also help you land the job. The most obvious part of this is who would be your boss if you worked here: Who is your Decision Maker? Everything you can find out about that person is potentially very useful in getting a job here. What are their expectations of people who work for them? Their interests? Their goals? Their likes and dislikes? The more you can find out the better.

It's also great to know who else is involved. Who would you be working with, directly and indirectly? What other people does the Decision Maker routinely relate to, in any department? Which of them have the Decision Maker's trust? Information on who the Decision Maker likes and trusts is not easy to get and you usually can't ask about it directly. But keep your ears open and ask a gentle question now and then.

TALK ABOUT YOUR PROFESSION WITH PROFESSIONAL PEERS

Conversations with your professional peers—those who are not Insiders at your targets—are another important category of Level Two conversations. With professional peers, the primary conversation is usually "talking shop." You should do that the way you always do it.

You talk about those areas of professional interest that are most important to you. You share information with your colleagues based on your past experience and on the research you have done as part of your job search.

These conversations with peers might also branch out into conversations about other organizations. This can be a logical flow of the conversation and very useful to you. It could lead to your sharing your entire Target List, collecting organizational information, and getting introductions to other Level Twos and even to Level Ones.

Level One Professional Contacts

Do not use your Target List.

Talk to Influencers if you can.

Get your message out, focused on this organization.

Look for an opportunity to meet the Decision Maker, even for a few minutes.

Level One professional contacts include Decision Makers, their bosses, and anyone else in a position to influence them. These people, of course, are the most important contacts of your job search. It often takes some work to reach them, and when you do, you want to do the best you can with them.

No matter who you are—a new grad, a senior executive, or anyone in between—you probably know very few appropriate Decision Makers. Or none.

After all, these are people who aren't normally part of your network. They might be older than you are and they might not travel in the same circles as you do. If you know any—previous bosses, for example—do your homework and go ahead and contact them. But if you're like most job hunters, these are mostly people you will be introduced to, not people you already know.

Remember those networking goals—collecting information, getting your message out, and meeting people? They still apply, all the way to the end. But at Level One they're a little different. Let's take a look at the whole thing, starting with Influencers.

Getting acquainted with and talking to the people who surround the Decision Maker can be as important as getting acquainted with the Decision Maker. Some of these people will influence the Decision Maker on hiring decisions. Any of them who are familiar with you, your interest, and what you have to offer can keep the possibility of hiring you fresh in the Decision Maker's mind. When the Decision Maker mentions the possibility of hiring someone, they can be the genius who has a candidate's name at the ready. Yours.

Since Level One contacts include the Decision Maker and people surrounding that person, your goal of getting your message out is particularly important here. Having Insiders at this level see you as a good candidate for current or future job openings is a major step toward an interview. You're in the right place, waiting for the right time. And now that you're talking to people inside the targeted organization, you should be able to tailor your message more closely to what this particular organization wants and needs.

I want to make sure that I'm not making you think that you need to become friends with dozens of people in the organization. You don't need to do that. But I do want to make sure you're aware how very useful any conversations with Insiders can be—even short conversations on the telephone. So look for opportunities, meet as many as you can, and follow up with them regularly. This is true of both Level One and Level Two Insiders.

And, of course, you're always looking for that ultimate networking goal, a conversation with the Decision Maker.

When you have an introduction to a Decision Maker—or know one that you can call directly—be careful. Use the opportunity wisely. Prepare carefully before approaching them. You may want to talk to some other contacts first as part of your preparation.

These cautions particularly apply to recent grads who are lucky enough to have parents who know one or more possible Decision Makers, or friends who have parents like that. Sometimes the parents want to make the introduction right now, immediately. But if you allow that to happen before you're prepared, you could end up looking like a rank amateur rather than a serious professional. You need to do your research first.

Even if you're an experienced senior business executive, similar advice applies. You may have easy access to other executives at and above your level. But don't talk to them until you're ready. You should research their company carefully, even if you have no intention of working there. You would also be smart to be well informed on their competitors, some of which are your targets, although you may not say so. That means doing Internet research, checking their Websites, annual reports, 10K's, executive bios, the whole thing. I mean, hey, you're an executive. You need to look and sound like one.

Look for a Sponsor

Any Level One or Two Insider who wants you to join the organization can be a sponsor.

A sponsor actively assists you with information, introductions, and advice.

Every now and then, a job hunter gets really lucky and finds a sponsor inside a target organization. This is an informal relationship and it's unusual for anyone to call it "sponsor," but that's what it is. It's someone other than the Decision Maker who wants to have you in the organization—someone at Level Two or One.

They might want you there simply because they're a friend of yours. But it could also be someone you recently met or have only a weak relationship with—maybe someone who shares your interests or values and is convinced they'd enjoy working with you. Or maybe someone who sees your skills as particularly useful. Or someone who sees you as a person they could easily get along with, someone who would be a great colleague and teammate, or an organizational ally in the executive suite.

A sponsor can be unusually helpful by giving you extensive inside information. Not proprietary information, of course, but simply the kind of information that will help you become a better and more effective candidate. Because they're inside the organization, they can help you make the right decisions on who to talk to and when.

They can also give you tips on what to say—and not say—to various Insiders, including the Decision Maker. A sponsor can draw a road map for you so you can see the best ways to get where you want to go inside their organization. If they are high enough or close to the Decision Maker, they can actively advocate hiring you.

I sometimes hear effective job hunters jokingly using the language of espionage about sponsors. They say, "I now have moles in four organizations." Or, "My operatives tell me that there are big changes coming up at...." But it's not really like spying. It's more like having a native guide in a foreign country, someone who knows the language and culture.

There's no guarantee that you'll find a sponsor in any of your targets, but keep your eyes and ears open. If someone seems especially supportive of your candidacy, don't be afraid to ask for a little help—the two of you could become allies.

Communication With Professional Contacts

Be interested at Level One and with any Insider.
Be interesting at Levels Three and Two.

Although there are a number of things you're working on at Level One, I'd say that the most important—and the easiest—is letting them know that you're interested. If you want to be convincing on that, of course, it has to be true. Your interest has to be backed up with knowledge of the organization and specific reasons why you're interested.

I've said this before, but it's worth emphasizing. Someone who is both knowledgeable about and interested in the job and organization is automatically a better candidate. This is particularly true at entry level, where no one has a lot of experience. But it's true at all levels of employment, right up to senior executives. Everyone likes to hire a candidate who really likes the organization and who really, *really* wants the job.

Imagine two candidates. One clearly has a burning interest in the job and organization but only moderate skills. The other has strong skills but shows very little interest. Seems a bit bored, even. Most employers would pick the first one. I would.

So at Level One and with any Insider, don't hesitate to express and demonstrate your interest in the organization and in working there. Repeatedly. Persistently. Unfailingly.

At Levels Three and Two, I'd say the most important thing is to be an interesting networking partner—someone people will want to talk to. This can take some work on your part. I don't know whether you'll need to do a lot of work in this level of professional networking or just a little. But as you talk to people, you'll find out.

In any case, your Internet and library research on organizations and issues affecting them is a critical part of your success. In your professional networking, you need to be a well-informed professional, not merely a job hunter. Let's take a closer look:

You're a More Interesting Professional Networking Partner When You Share Information Regarding:

Industries and organizations.
People in those organizations.
Best practices in your profession.

There are three ways you can be more interesting in networking conversations with other professionals. These three apply any time your relationship with your networking partner is purely professional. They are all about using "pure networking" in job search, networking without a pre-existing personal relationship or community.

Because networking is about information exchange between people who share common interests, your most important preparation is having information to *give* as well as information you want to gather. The best kind of information for you to share is on topics that your professional networking partners will find interesting, useful, and valuable. So it needs to be work-related information.

The three main categories of information you can share in a job search are information on organizations, information on people, and professional information. All of these make you a more interesting networking partner, someone people will look forward to talking to. Let's look at each.

SHARING INFORMATION ON INDUSTRIES AND ORGANIZATIONS

If you are conducting an effective job search, you have a Target List of organizations you want to work for. This list is organized into categories, such as Health Care, for example, or Systems Consultants or Banking. Part of your job in job hunting is to research the categories—as well as the individual organizations in each category that particularly interest you.

The information you find will help you make good decisions about which opportunities to pursue. It will also make you a more appealing candidate and more effective in the interview. And that same information will make you more interesting to your professional networking contacts—especially those currently working in the categories you are researching.

Businesspeople, for example, are usually very interested in what their competitors are doing. Some of those competitors are on your list. You've read their Websites, checked them on blogs, and Googled them for articles. And you have learned about them from talking to others. You probably have information that your networking partner doesn't have. If you pass it on and tell them where they can find more, you've done them a favor, and made yourself more interesting to talk to.

But it's not just about competitors. It's also about which organizations are doing what and how they're doing it. It's about what the trends are, the opportunities and challenges the trends present, and how organizations are working with them. This kind of "industry news" is something most professionals and managers are interested in. If you're a reliable source of that kind of information, you're interesting to talk to—maybe even more than once—and someone they might want to introduce you to their friends and colleagues.

SHARING INFORMATION ON PEOPLE

In talking about organizations, it's only natural to move to a discussion of the people in those organizations, the "who's-doing-what-over-there" part. When you read an article about an organization, it will often mention one or more people. Journalists write articles by interviewing people. They identify the people they quote, usually mentioning their job titles and where they work. You can research those people and perhaps even find bios on them.

I'm not suggesting that you indulge in name-dropping. When you talk about people you don't know, I think you should mention that you don't know them. But if you know how to use the Internet even just a little, you can be as well informed on people as you are on organizations. Once again, this makes you more interesting to talk to.

I am most definitely not suggesting that you indulge in gossip. If you are job hunting, gossip might get some people to talk to you. But when it comes to actual hiring, no one wants to hire a person who can't control their mouth. It's dangerous. They know that if you gossip about others, you will sooner or later gossip about them. So stay with positive information on who is doing what, for whom, and how. Stay away from things that are negative or too personal to be included in a professional conversation.

In every networking conversation you have, you can learn more about organizations on your list and people who work at them. So the longer you are networking, the more information you have to share and the more interesting a networking partner you become.

SHARING PROFESSIONAL INFORMATION

An even more sophisticated approach is sharing professional information, information that can directly help your networking partners do their jobs better.

It works like this: You start by selecting an area (or more than one area) of knowledge related to your profession, one that you would like to know more about and one that you hope and expect will be part of your next job. It might be related to best professional practices in your field.

For example, a senior manager might choose leadership theories. A salesperson might have an interest in software and hardware that support contact management. A public school teacher might be interested in educational approaches used in high performing schools around the country or studies on how test scores correlate with retention of learning.

You then research that topic on the Internet and in the library. Because you select a topic that's not too broad, you can become quite knowledgeable in a short time. As you discuss it with others, you become even more knowledgeable. Again, you become a more interesting networking partner. And you become a more appealing candidate, someone knowledgeable about your profession, someone who takes the time to learn what's happening in the field.

As you do this research, you'll notice that journalists writing on the topic of your interest will quote people in organizations. When those people are relevant to your search, you may want to contact them, as well as talk about them. If you can't get an introduction, you can use the article as a point of common interest and call them directly. This move crosses the line into the cool zone, but it's a move where the odds are pretty good because of the narrow and clearly defined shared interest.

You can use the professional information you collect as part of connecting with Level Three and Two professional contacts, with language something like this:

I've been reading up on leadership theory, especially as it applies to creating change in large organizations. I've taken a look at classics like Drucker, but also at some more recent, less well-known writers. Some things in the books are exactly the same things that I've seen some top managers at top companies in our industry doing.

I've been taking a good look at contact management software and which PDA's and cell phones are best for salespeople. I've made lists of the pros and cons of each.

I've been looking at some of the educational approaches being used by award-winning schools around the country. I'd be happy to share some of that if you're interested.

These are all possible conversation starters as well as offers of helpful information. When you find networking partners interested in the topic, you can follow up by sending them articles, Internet links, or even books. The shared interest can help keep the conversation going.

Another topic that most professionals are interested in is career management and job hunting. Although this isn't strictly professional information, sometimes it's a good topic. Some of your networking partners will be interested in what you've learned about conducting a systematic, professional and, highly effective job search. Many people are concerned about losing their jobs these days, especially in the business world, and are thinking about their next job search—whether they're willing to admit it or not.

The main point with your professional contacts is one you already heard: it's particularly important that you make them comfortable. You can do this by the conversation topics you select. With professional contacts, it might be better to start by offering them information, rather than asking for information. Once the conversation is moving, you can both give and get information.

This is a different approach from the one you use with personal contacts. You cannot expect professional contacts to be interested in assisting you. They might be, but you can't rely on that. You may need to make it more of a two-way street, offering them information of value, and giving as much as you get.

So rather than leading off with discussion of your job search and your Target List, you focus more on shared interests—industry, trends, people, professional information—and signal that you have information to share. And, of course, you get the strongest introduction you can.

On the other hand, it's also important to let them know that you're in a job search, because that will also be part of the conversation. Some job hunters fail to do that and the results can be problematic. The potential networking partner could be confused about your intentions.

Your success with professional contacts depends on your choice of which ones to talk to, your preparation for those talks, and your handling of them when you get there. With some attention to these three kinds of information, organizational, people, and professional, you can make a positive impression on practically everyone—and keep your search moving very effectively.

You are always looking for introductions to new professional contacts. The key, as always, is information sharing around common interests. Here, as with personal contacts, you should always consider using questions such as:

- *Who might know more about this?*

- *Do you think she might be interested in the information I have?*

- *Do you think he and I should get acquainted?*

USE THE LANGUAGE OF THE PROFESSION AND INDUSTRY

While exchanging information with professional contacts, you need to speak their language. If you're exploring industries in which you have never worked, it's important to learn the language early on. When you're talking to Insiders, you should speak the language of that organization as much as possible.

For example, do the people who work at United Amalgamated Incorporated call the place UA? UAI? United? If they all call it UA and you do too, you sound like you fit right in. But if you call it UAI and no one ever uses that name, you won't make the best impression.

There is also a wide range of professional and industry-specific lingo that is familiar to Insiders and part of their normal conversation. This includes acronyms, unusual phrases, and special definitions for common words. And of course, mis-using any of this is a faux pas.

If your luck is bad, no one will tell you about the mis-step you're making. So check out the language on their Website and by talking to Threes who are familiar with them. Learn the key words and lingo your targets use, so you can discuss their issues in their language. Then keep your ears open for refinements when talking to Level Twos and Ones. Your skilled use of the language makes you a more appealing candidate.

If you're a recent grad or a career changer, this is even more important because you have more to learn. You may need to learn the language of a new profession as well as a new industry. But don't worry. Most entry level candidates don't bother to do it at all. If you put any attention to learning the language, you'll look better than average right off the bat. When in doubt about the correct terminology, ask.

Once you have used the Internet and the library to expand your knowledge of organizations, people, and professional issues, you're ready to talk to Level Three and Two professional contacts. Getting in touch with professional contacts is different from personal contacts. Let's take a look at making initial contact with professionals.

Professional Contacts Want to Know:

Who is calling?
What is it about?

Phone calls at work are handled differently from personal phone calls. At the beginning of a work call—especially with someone they don't know—most people want to know who is calling and the purpose of the call. Normally, the "who" part is answered with a name, job title, and organizational affiliation.

People want to know the purpose of the call in order to prepare themselves for the conversation—or to decide if they want to have the conversation at all. Sometimes it's smart to answer this question even when it isn't asked.

In making job-hunting calls to professional contacts, it's important to let them know as soon as possible that you are not going to make them uncomfortable. As we've discussed, unemployment makes people uncomfortable, and—whether you're employed or not—people may be concerned that they will have to say no to a likable and deserving job hunter.

Add all of this up, and it's clear that how you begin your telephone calls with professional contacts is important. Let's take a look at a sample script.

Suppose that you are Pat Person, a marketing manager formerly employed by United Amalgamated. You have an introduction to a professional peer.

Script: Calling a Professional Peer Who Is Not at a Target Company

You: Good morning. This is Pat Person. I'm calling at the suggestion of Jack Landis. Like you, I'm a marketing director, formerly with United Amalgamated. I've been doing some research on the most effective uses of Internet advertising. Jack thought you might be interested in hearing about it.

Them: What kind of research have you done?

You: I've identified the seven most effective uses of Internet advertising. In addition to Jack, I've talked to five other marketing directors as well as a couple of professors at the Walcott B-school. Jack and the others have collaborated with me on listing out the pros and cons of each. I'd like to discuss the whole thing with you, so I'm calling to see when we might be able to get together.

Them: You said that you're "formerly" with United Amalgamated?

You: Yes, my entire department was let go in that big downsizing following the merger. So I'm looking for the right new spot. I'm doing some networking I probably should've done a long time ago. I have great respect for your company, but no reason to believe that your company is the right place for me—at least not right now. I have a couple of dozen others that I'm pursuing. But Jack thought you and I might enjoy meeting each other. May I take you to lunch?

Them: I'm always interested in connecting with professional peers. I think it's good career management for all of us in marketing management to know each other and see how we can be resources to each other.

You: That's exactly why Jack and I got together and why he thought you and I might enjoy talking. May I take you to lunch?

Them: Yes. I'd like to hear what you've got on Internet advertising. And I think the world of Jack. He's great. How about next Tuesday?

In this example, we've assumed that you have both information to share and an introduction. It's possible to get started with only one of those. Sometimes, when there's a strong connection between the person who introduced you and the new person, an introduction is all it takes. You set up an appointment and get off the phone.

With professional contacts you've never met, meeting them in person is highly desirable and usually well worth the cost of a breakfast or lunch. In that case, it's usually better to stay on the phone only as long as it takes to make the appointment.

In this kind of meeting, you'll be sharing information about organizations, people, and your profession—and looking for introductions to new people. The easiest way to get those introductions is simply to ask.

Ask for Introductions

In conversations with professional contacts, you are always listening for them to mention relevant names, names of people with whom you might have common interests. Just as you do with personal contacts, you can ask if an introduction makes sense at the moment when the name is mentioned. Or you can collect the names during the conversation and ask about some or all of them all at once at the end.

Doing it at the end usually makes more sense, because it allows the two of you to select the most appropriate of the names mentioned. And because asking each time a name is mentioned might discourage them from mentioning names.

Once you have agreement that an introduction makes sense, you might want to ask for additional information about the people you're being introduced to. The simplest way is, *"Can you tell me a little more about them?"*

In talking to professional contacts, remember that you may be doing them a favor. At the Decision Maker level, they get the opportunity to take a look at a possible job candidate without paying a fee or taking a lot of time. At the Decision Maker level or below, your networking partner may be able to pass you on to someone who is looking to hire, in their organization, or another one.

At the right moment, your contact can be the hero who produced a great job candidate—you—without a huge headhunter fee or a protracted candidate search. You should also know that people who are thinking this way probably won't mention it to you.

When you sometimes have meetings where you get no new introductions, don't be concerned. Even if you don't meet the Decision Maker—or anyone new—getting your message out is effective and important. And the closer to the Decision Maker you disseminate it, the more likely that the Decision Maker will hear it.

Sooner or later, your Level Three and Two networking conversations will produce introductions to Level One contacts—especially if you remember to ask for them. Once you've learned the appropriate Decision Maker's name, the standard procedure is not complicated. The most obvious way to go is:

"I'd really like to meet Mr./Ms._____ . I understand that they aren't hiring right now, but sooner or later they will need someone. When that day comes, I would really like to be that person. I'm very interested and believe I could make a real contribution. Would you be willing to introduce me?"

Your request for an introduction to a Decision Maker is even stronger when you can point to a common interest, so it's smart to research them. When you have been able to find something out about a Decision Maker before meeting them, you are also more likely to have a productive conversation when you do meet.

Connecting With Decision Makers Is Easier When You've Researched Them

Get their names and titles.

Check the Internet for background information about them.

Talk to networking partners about them.

Map their networks.

Making connections with Level One professional contacts is the ultimate goal of job-search networking. It's something you should start thinking about early on, when you're first making your Target List. The question is always, "Who are the right Decision Makers and how can I make contact with them in a way that's comfortable for both of us?"

The first step, of course, is identifying target organizations. The second step is identifying who your next boss would be if you worked there. You want that person's name and exact title. You can sometimes get that information by cold-calling the organization and asking, as well as by networking.

Checking the Internet or the library for background information is the third step. If you're a senior manager who will report to a top executive, your Decision Makers will often be listed in directories and databases. And you may have easy access to their bios as well. They have probably been written about in journal articles or in business news published in newspapers or on the Web. And they may have written things themselves. All of this makes it very likely that you'll get some good information on the Internet.

For any job hunter, the fourth step and last of researching your Decision Makers will be most effectively done in conversations with your networking partners. The initial Internet research, as usual, primes the pump. Then you begin including the topic in your networking conversations. By mentioning the right people by name and asking about them, you can get very useful information, and maybe even an introduction.

For this reason, it can be smart to have a column on your Target List where you list the appropriate Decision Maker's name and title. At the outset, that column will be mostly blank. But the blank column opens conversations with your personal contacts and Level Three professional contacts. If you have a good guess on the job titles your Decision Makers are likely to have, they may know some of the names immediately. And they might also be willing to ask around for you, to collect names and locate possible intermediaries to connect you with those people.

Along with the names, you're gathering professional and relevant personal information on Decision Makers. Where did they work early on? What were their past jobs and employers? Where did they attend college? What degree do they have? What are their non-work interests? Do they play tennis? Golf? What church or synagogue are they a member of? What professional groups?

In collecting this information, you're looking for common interests, because that's what fuels networking. Did that person attend State U., like you did? Do you share an interest in collecting Eastern European postage stamps? Are you both Roman Catholic? African American? Did you both once live in Williston, North Dakota?

Any shared interest helps, and the more of them you find, the more possible conversation topics you have. And the more likelihood that the two of you will "hit it off" when you meet and the commonalities are known. It helps move you out of the cool zone and into a warmer place. Sometimes you will use this information directly. In cases where mentioning it might be indiscreet, it still gives you important clues on how to behave.

MAP THEIR NETWORKS

This information will also help you with the fifth and last step of researching Decision Makers: sketching out a map of their networks as we discussed in Chapter Five. This is a proposition that involves some guesswork, but it's always worth a try because it can speed your search. You may have networking contacts that are particularly good at this exercise, people who can help you with it.

What you're looking for, of course, are the places where their networks intersect with yours. Or at least for logical entrance points into their networks, so you can reach them with an introduction or two—

at the second or third degree of separation. A simple example is that you discover that they graduated from your university. Or that they live on the same block as your cousin. Or that they are a member of your best friend's church. Or that they are active in your chapter of the Society of Human Resource Managers.

See what you can do to map the networks of people you want to reach. Not just Decision Makers, but anyone you want to get through to. Look for where your network intersects with theirs. Look for people in their networks that could be intermediaries. As you'll see in the next chapter, social networking Websites might help with this. Sometimes this is the kind of thing we talked about with Level Threes— sales reps or consultants. Or it could be simply someone you both know. You may find that some people are easier to reach than you thought.

Once you have information and an introduction, you're ready to call the Decision Maker.

Decision Makers Want to Know:

What's in it for me?

What do you want from me?

Is this going to be awkward or difficult?

How long will it take and will it be worth that amount of time?

Decision Makers are people with less time, and the higher they are the more carefully they need to manage their time. So they may be more reluctant to set up meetings without a good reason. Of course they want to know who's calling and what it's about. But they may want to know more than that.

Although most would not ask directly, they probably want to know what benefit they're likely to get from a meeting. They may have many people wanting their time or their assistance with a wide range of things that may or may not relate to their job. Questions such as,

"What's in it for me?" "What do you want?" and "How long will it take?" are likely to be on their mind. When you're calling them, you're smart to answer those questions even if they're not asked.

Suppose again that you are Pat Person, the marketing manager formerly employed by United Amalgamated. You have talked to professional peers and Insiders at one of your targets. Now you have an introduction to the Decision Maker, a CEO whom you have never met.

Script: Calling a Decision Maker With an Introduction

You: Good morning. This is Pat Person. I'm a marketing director, calling at the suggestion of Jennifer Johnson. She said you might be interested in the research I'm doing on the seven most effective uses of Internet advertising.

Them: Jennifer mentioned you. How do you happen to know her?

You: Jennifer and I were classmates when we were undergrads at Walcott. We were in the same dorm. Last year, we worked together on the Walcott capital campaign. I really enjoy working with her.

Them: I certainly feel the same way. She was among the best financial managers I ever had. I was sorry to lose her, but her new job is a big step up and I couldn't match it. You said you're a marketing director. Where do you work?

You: Right now I'm between jobs. I left UA after the merger. Quite frankly, one of the places that I would most like to work is your company. I've heard great things about it from Jennifer and others. I have no reason to believe that you'd have a job for me right now, but the next time you need someone in marketing I'm very interested.

Meanwhile, I thought the information on Internet advertising might be useful to you. I have talked to marketing directors at six different companies about it and collected pros and cons on each option. I've also been talking to a couple of professors at Walcott about it. I think that three or four of the options might be useful to you and I'd like to tell you about them in person. May I take you to lunch?

Them: I'm pretty solidly booked at lunchtime. Is it something you could cover in 20 minutes?

You: Absolutely.

Them: I'm going to transfer you back to my assistant to set up an appointment. I'm looking forward to talking to you. Please give my best to Jennifer the next time you see her.

You: I will. Thank you.

You don't know if you got the appointment because of Jennifer, Walcott (which you knew to be the CEO's alma mater), the Internet advertising information, or some plans the CEO has but is not ready to reveal. And of course, you don't really care what the reason was. Your job is to give someone the best reasons you can. Then you get a yes or a no.

If you get a no when you request for a meeting with a Decision Maker, you have nonetheless made important progress in your search. This CEO has now heard of you, talked to you for a few minutes, and is aware of your area of expertise as well as some shared interests. You should continue to follow up with this person regularly. If you later find another, better reason for a meeting, why not try again?

Always Give Them Your Resume. Afterward.

With professional contacts, just like personal contacts, always give them your resume. But don't lead with it. Handing someone your resume at the outset tends to convey the message, "I need a job right now." This often gets people thinking about job openings or who's hiring. Or it throws them into the myths we talked about in Chapter

Two. None of these are useful, and some will be a step backward. So don't lead with your resume.

The rule of thumb is to give your professional contacts your resume after you talk to them, just as you do with personal contacts. You can give it to them on paper at the end of a meeting or e-mail it to them as a follow-up. Or both.

Give them your Core Message verbally at the beginning of the conversation—and get the conversation pointed in a useful direction. If they ask to see your resume, of course, you'll give them a copy when they ask. You're always carrying a few copies, right?

If they say they'll pass your resume on to others, of course that's useful. But if they're willing to introduce you to the people that they'd pass the resume on to, that's even better.

We've now covered nearly all of the "Talk" part of the Decide-Prepare-Talk-Land sequence we discussed in Chapter Two.

Before we move on to "Land," Chapter Nine will discuss seven tools and strategies that can take your job-search networking from effective to highly effective. And, of course, we'll check in with Ben.

One more thing: Now that we've covered the professional networking part, I want to remind you that you might never do it. Some job hunters jump directly from personal contacts to a Decision Maker and move quickly into landing a new job. I hope you'll be one of those.

ORVILLE'S JOURNAL

Star Players Have to Work Harder

"Jess made me come over," Ben plopped down into the sofa in my office. "She wants to make sure I talk to you enough. So I don't mess up."

"You've been depressed again?"

"No, I'm on a roll. My search is on cruise control. But it never hurts to talk to a great coach, right?"

"Well, that's a better way to get started." I moved from the desk to the rocker. "How about some tea?"

"Okay," he said, reaching for the teapot, "But don't you think a top flight coach should have a cooler with some great micro-brewery stuff in it?"

"No, actually, I think the star player should have that kind of thing when he invites the coach over to shoot some pool. Along with jasmine tea, of course."

"You're right. I've been neglecting you. How about some eight ball tonight? Seven-thirty?"

"Now you're talking. Yes. And let's get on with the coaching, because I've got 40 more pages to edit today."

Ben sipped his tea for a minute, then launched into it. "The two Decision Maker conversations went well. One was a lunch. I like both of them and their companies. One would be a relocation."

"Good."

"Second, I had my meeting with Rachel. She's amazing. She had prepared a list of 26 possible contacts. We spent an hour talking about them. We picked out 14. She's going to e-mail all of them. We talked about what I'll say to each one. I made notes on it. I'm starting today."

"That's outstanding. She's a major ally, isn't she?"

"Yes. She's a good friend, too. She's really going out of her way. When this is over, I'm going to buy her a really nice thank-you present."

"Good. What else?"

"So I come home from the Rachel meeting, and Jessie says, 'I can do that too.' So we go through her entire social networking site and look at all of her contacts. She had already given me 11. We found 37 more. We picked eight to start with. I'll get to them next week."

"Great. What else?"

"Well, this is going to sound kinda dumb, but I haven't gone through my own contacts as carefully as Rachel did with hers. So I started doing that. I got the whole daggone list printed out. I'm really taking a close look at each one. Picking the best ones to get going with, instead of just going at it random."

"That's good to get systematic about it. But I hope you'll include some of the odd ones sometimes, too. You never know who knows who until you ask. What else?"

"What else? Isn't that enough?"

"It's more than enough. You're doing great. But if a guy can rush for 50 yards, why wouldn't the coach see if he could do 100?"

"Well, okay, there *is* one more thing. I've been doing the Chapter Nine stuff. I've set up a database. I'm improving my Internet presence. Getting all the right keywords in my profiles and cleaning it up some. And follow-up."

"Good. What are you doing with follow-up?"

"I set up a system of follow-up reminders. I'm re-contacting all Decision Makers every three weeks. And other people at various intervals. I'm keeping notes on all conversations. I've even put a summary of my meeting with Jessie in the database."

"Your wife is in your database? Now you've gone too far—even for me. You're beyond effective. You might even be over the edge."

"*Over the Edge Job Hunting*." Ben smiled. "I think that's your next book, Orville." He finished his tea and headed for the door.

"No, that's *your* book. But maybe I'll be your co-author. I'd sure rather see job hunters do too much than too little."

Ben stopped at the door and turned around. "Wait," he said, "There's one more thing. I forgot to tell you about my conversation with Alicia."

"The one you had a couple of weeks ago?"

"It was 18 days ago, actually. She asked me if I'd consider consulting. I said yes. Was that a mistake?"

"No. It's my favorite answer, actually. And follow up the 'yes' with a question. 'Yes of course I'd consider it. Why do you ask?' The 'why' part can open doors."

"Well, Coach, that's exactly what I did. I asked the 'Why do you ask?' question. It got me referrals to two former engineering professors that she hadn't mentioned. They're both consultants now."

"See that?" I was laughing out loud now. "You *are* capable of 100 yards in a game."

"But I don't want to be a consultant."

"Fine. Go talk to them anyway. See what happens."

"Okay." Ben stepped through the door. Then he turned around again. "Now you're going to be looking for 150 yards, aren't you?"

Looping Ahead

Staying Systematic

Social Networking Websites

Networking Groups

Out of Town and International

The Consulting Strategy

The Other Six

| DECIDE | PREPARE | **TALK** | LAND |

Chapter Nine

Networking Tools and Advanced Strategies

We've been talking all along about a strategic approach to highly effective networking, and now we're going to push that a little further. If you do the things we've talked about so far, you'll be highly effective in your job search networking—well above average. If you also add some of the things suggested in this chapter, well my goodness, who knows how good you could get?

I say "*some* of the things in this chapter" because I don't expect everyone to use all of them. Consulting, for example, is not for everyone. But I included it because some people will effectively use it as part of their search.

On the other hand, I think everyone should do the first two things on the list, Looping Ahead and Staying Systematic. "Looping Ahead" is about looping back to people you've already talked to in order to move your search ahead. It's an easy way to make networking more effective, and it's also just plain good manners, so we'll take it up first.

Second, we'll take a look at staying systematic in job hunting. I'm well aware that some people see being systematic as an important part of anything they do. These people always want things organized and are uncomfortable when they're not. My wife is in this category, and when you want to get something done, you're lucky to have her around.

Of course, there are also people who regard organization and systems as a necessary evil. These folks organize things when they have to. The rest of the time, they prefer to just flow with events as they unfold. They might see networking as a natural, almost organic process with its own internal logic. Which can be a useful way to see it.

But in job-search networking, some organization is necessary. So we'll look at some of the most important things to be systematic about. You'll find your own best way of handling it. You don't know how long your search will take, and the longer it turns out to be, the happier you'll be that you set up some systems at the outset.

Then we'll take a look at social networking Websites, the ones that began with Friendster, Facebook, and LinkedIn, and have now expanded well beyond those old originals and how they could help in job-search networking. If you don't use any, now might be a good time to start. They can speed your networking. They're also a useful ongoing career management tool—if you know how to use them that way. Your Internet presence can also affect job hunting.

Next, we'll look at those networking groups for job hunters that have been popular for many years now. They can be beneficial, but as we discussed in Chapter Three, the myths chapter, they're not the only place you can network. We'll look at how to best use these groups, if you do decide to use one.

If you're conducting a job hunt in two or more geographic locations, you'll want to think about how to best do that kind of "out-of-town" networking. I'm often asked about this one and I'll provide some step-by-step suggestions. The same principles apply to networking internationally.

Finally, we'll take a quick look at the consulting strategy, a way to hedge your bets while taking a slightly different approach to networking, and at the other six job-hunting techniques that you should consider using along with networking.

Let's get started.

Looping Back to Move Ahead

Go back to people you already talked to.

Give them a progress report.

See if they have any further information or referrals.

Effective job hunters talk to most of their networking contacts more than once. At the end of the job search, if you go over the records of who the job hunter talked to, you will always find that there are many more conversations than there are people. This is because effective job hunters keep all of their networking partners well informed by having successive conversations with each person.

Imagine yourself being on the receiving end. A personal contact, a good friend, discusses their job search with you. You make two or three suggestions and a couple of referrals to other people. Weeks go by. You don't hear from your friend. You don't know what's happening. Did they find a job? Did any of your suggestions work? Did they talk to the referrals? Did it go well? Or did they maybe ignore everything you told them?

In my opinion, it's just plain impolite not to loop back to a contact who offered assistance and suggestions. This does not mean that you have to accept all of their suggestions. But most people will be interested to know what happened next. If you keep them informed, you also keep them involved in your job search project. Some of your personal contacts might be very interested in being a partner to you throughout the search, if you give them the opportunity.

I recommend returning to some of your personal contacts again and again through the course of your search. Each time you report back to them on what happened, they may also have new ideas, suggestions, and referrals for you. After all, your search continues to evolve. Your Target List grows and changes. It's an ongoing conversation.

In reporting back—as with anything in your job search—be as positive as possible. Emphasize your successes and build on them.

And always use the next contact as an opportunity to express your gratitude for what the last conversation gave you. Even though you thanked them at the time, the second thank-you is more meaningful, because you can now tell them what came of the original meeting.

For example, if your friend Susan gave you information on several of your targets and introduced you to two new people, you might return to her later to say something like this:

Script: An Update Conversation With a Networking Partner

Susan, I wanted to get back to you and let you know how much I appreciated your introducing me to George. He was a gold mine of information on my targets, just as you said he might be. He gave me great information on eight of them and introduced me to Insiders at three of those.

I really enjoyed talking to him. I can see why you like him. He has a great sense of humor. I also discovered that he and I share an interest in American history. We're both big readers of historical novels and biographies of historical figures. So we had a great talk about that too.

I've set up appointments to talk to two of the Insiders he introduced me to. One, Francine Ebell, works in my number one target. She's not in the exact area where I want to work, but she certainly knows about it and probably has friends there. We're having lunch, so we'll have plenty of time to talk.

I have a telephone appointment with another one, Paul Henry. He's actually in the department that I'm interested in at another target.

So I can't thank you enough. What you gave me was very useful. Based on my talks with George and some other people, I've updated my Target List. I have a number of new companies on it now. I'd like to send you the new list.

If I e-mail it, would you be willing to take a look and see if you have any other ideas or any other people I should talk to?

You might not do it all in one big long speech like that. It would probably be a back-and-forth conversation. But it's important not only to thank your original contact, but also to give them the details of what happened.

The details will let them know exactly how they were helpful. The details might also lead to additional information. For example, by mentioning that George introduced you to Francine and Paul, you open the door to getting more information on those two people. Perhaps your original contact even knows them.

After you talk to Francine and Paul, you may decide to report back to Susan—as well as George—on those conversations. In each of your follow-up conversations with Susan, you need to make a judgment about whether you are comfortable asking her for further assistance or whether you simply want to report back and leave the door open for her to offer something. And, of course, you need to consider what she would be comfortable with.

Please notice that in the report back to Susan, the second referral that Susan made was never mentioned. If that meeting did not go very well or did not result in anything, omitting mention of it is one possibility. If Susan asks about it, you can discuss it. Or, you might decide to raise the topic yourself and ask Susan to help you figure out what you could have done—or might still do—to make the contact more productive.

As you do this kind of looping back, some of your networking partners will actually become job-hunting partners, members of your team. When you land that great new job, some of them will be almost as happy about it as you are. They'll share your little successes along the way as well as the big success at the end.

With professional contacts, you may not take the process as far as you do with personal contacts. But you should definitely loop back to them to thank them and give them a report. It might be good to be brief and more businesslike.

With all of them, of course, a real-time conversation, on the telephone or in person, is your best chance of getting further information and additional referrals. In some cases, though, you'll decide to do it with an e-mail or a voice mail. And sometimes a handwritten note is the way to go, because they're so rare these days.

Some professional contacts may get just as involved as personal contacts. But there will certainly be others who will not, and it's usually better not to be too aggressive with them. Just thank them and leave them with a good impression of you.

The basic "standard procedure" with both personal and professional contacts is the same: thank them at the end of the first conversation you have with them, then re-contact them after you have taken action on any of their suggestions. On the second contact, thank them again and give them some details on the positive results of what they gave you, and see if they might have additional information or referrals for you. If so, you repeat the cycle.

The other thing you should do is keep a record of every contact with every networking partner.

Be Systematic About Keeping Records On:

Your contacts.

Your conversations.

Targeted organizations.

If your luck is good and your job search turns out to be shorter than average, you won't need a recordkeeping system. You might have a few dozen conversations, all in a few weeks. You will remember them well enough to be effective.

On the other hand, if your search turns out to be longer than average, you will have hundreds of conversations during a period of months. Yes, that's right, hundreds. Many will be repeat conversations with the same people. I hope that they will all be comfortable and perhaps even enjoyable. And I hope that in the end, the job you find will be excellent and well worth the effort. But if your search turns out to be longer than average, you will have a large number of conversations with a large number of people.

Most job hunters, of course, are somewhere between these two extremes. And most job hunters definitely need some kind of recordkeeping system. The kind of system you use is entirely up to you. There are numerous possibilities and I am not going to attempt to describe all of them, but I will make some suggestions on what your system needs to do for you. I encourage you to set one up right now. Please do not wait until you're a month into your search. Having the right setup at the beginning will save you time later.

RECORD BASIC CONTACT INFORMATION

First, you need to have records of all of the people you talked to, your networking partners. To start with the obvious, you need a record of the name, e-mail address, telephone number, and possibly street address of each of your networking partners. If they are professional contacts, you also want the correct job title and organizational affiliation.

This can be as simple as updating your address book or autodial each time you talk to someone new—whether that first conversation goes anywhere or not. With a PDA or database, you may have space for considerably more information. Because you don't know where conversations might later go, the rule of thumb is "more is better."

If you also record additional information on each person, it can make future networking conversations easier. It can also give you the opportunity to be of service to your networking partners by passing on information that might be helpful to them. In this category are things such as work and non-work interests, personal and family information (such as the names of other family members), the names of previous employers, and any other information you happen to pick up in conversations.

It might be smart to record some of this information even with your friends. You already know the names of their family members and many of their interests. But you may not ordinarily talk about their past work experience. And remembering that could be useful.

KEEP RECORDS OF WHAT YOU BOTH SAID

The second kind of information that needs to be recorded is the content of each and every conversation. This is most important with Insiders and Decision Makers, your Level Two and One professional contacts. In talking to this group, you could be very close to your next job. You want to remember everything they tell you and the main points of what you said to them. This information can turn out to be very useful in later conversations.

So, make notes after each conversation. If it's a lunch or a visit in the workplace, find a quiet place to sit down immediately after you leave the meeting. Write down everything you can remember about the conversation. Include everything you learned about the organization and other people. Also, include any personal information that was mentioned, so when Harry later mentions Chippie, you'll know that's his dog, not his wife.

If the networking conversation is on the telephone, you can take notes as you talk. If you're going to do this with a keyboard, be sure that the keyboard cannot be heard over the telephone. Test it with a friend to make sure, or type your notes after the call.

You should make notes on conversations with personal contacts, too, even conversations with friends. Do it alone after the meeting, not during the meeting, unless it's to note a name, someone's job title, or another important fact. With personal contacts, you don't need as much detail in your notes. But you certainly want to remember who you thanked and what you followed up on. And you want to remember who introduced you to whom.

KEEP A FILE ON EACH TARGETED ORGANIZATION

The third kind of information you want to record is information on organizations. You may want a separate file—paper or electronic—for each of your target organizations. In this file, you will keep information on the organization and the people who work there.

These files on organizations will let you see what progress you're making with each organization on your Target List. You can review them from time to time to see what you need to do next. Even more important, this information will enable you to do a great job at an interview—or with that unexpected telephone call from an Insider.

If you are someone who does networking professionally, as part of your job, you may already have contact tracking software which does everything we have talked about and more. If you're a spreadsheet or database user, one of them might be a good choice. If you are tech savvy, you probably already know what hardware and software you will use. And if you're not tech savvy, don't worry. You can do everything you need to do with a three-ring binder and a pen.

Whether you're tech savvy or not, you should give some thought to the place the Internet will play in your job search.

Your Three Most Important Internet Activities

Evaluate your Internet presence.

Use social networking Websites.

Do Internet research.

If you haven't Googled yourself recently, please set the book down and go do that right now. Use a couple of search engines, not just Google. I'll wait for you here.

What did you find? How many reasons to hire you showed up in your search? How many reasons to cross you off of the finalist list?

I asked you to do that because your next employer will probably do it. They will probably do it as part of the screening process before they hire you. If they see things that scare them off, they won't hire you. They'll probably just quietly stop talking to you. If they see things that confirm the good impression they already have of you, then you move up the list. They may not admit to checking you out this way. But they probably will. I would.

Some of your networking contacts will also check you out on the Internet. Some people will decide whether they want to meet you or not based on what they find on the Web—text and photos both.

Many GenXers and Millenials have lived most of their lives on the Internet. If you are in one of those generations, you and other people may have posted a great deal of information about you over the years (and misinformation as well). If you are now looking for a job, you need to look from the employer's point of view at everything the Internet has to say about you. Is it a positive message, one that supports your candidacy? If not, you may need to take some things down and ask other people to do the same.

Keep in mind that someone checking you out on the Internet might contact people they find on any Web page about you. So look at all of your social networking Websites. Are there people listed as your "friends" that you really don't know? People who might say the wrong thing if they got a phone call or an e-mail?

If Internet searches about you produce nothing, then you have no Internet presence. Many members of the Baby Boom generation are still in this category. No harm done, but no good either. If this is you, you may want to establish a presence as part of your job search. The easiest and most useful way to do this is a social networking site, especially one built for career-related networking. The first large one in this category, of course, was LinkedIn. Now there are a wide range of choices. No matter which career-related site you use, the principles are the same.

A positive Internet presence is useful for job hunters, and a career-related social networking site is a great way to establish one. What you post there should be consistent with your resume and with everything that you are saying about yourself in your job hunting. Your posting is also an opportunity to include things that didn't make the cut on your resume. Any extra experience or skills can be included. Be sure to include keywords that employers might use in a search. And make sure there's nothing at all that might worry Decision Makers in your targeted organizations.

Of course, you can use more than one social networking site. Maybe you have been using a site designed only for social purposes. If so, you'd be smart to add a career-related site now. If you're in business, some sites are strongly oriented that way. If you're an executive, there are sites built just for you. And there are numerous other niche sites built around shared interests.

If you use more than one social networking site, make sure the message is consistent in all of them. If you wanted to go farther, you could put up a Website or start a blog. Those two—especially blogging—can be very time consuming, and may not be worth the effort for the returns that you'll get in job search. If you're currently employed and job hunting, I'd suggest registering at a social networking site and putting your time into networking rather than blogging.

The next step is to use your social networking Website in networking. If you're new to it, you will need to invite people in your network to connect with you on the site. In doing that, the more people you invite, the better—but they all need to be people you know and are comfortable talking with. Inviting them can be an opportunity to get back in touch with people you know but haven't been in touch with for a while, your dormant contacts.

You may want to have pages on more than one site, at least while you're job hunting. If many of your contacts are on site B, it makes no sense to invite them all to the site A where you are. They'll have to set up a new page. So go to them. Set up a page on site B and invite them to link with you there. The point is simple: do whatever you can to make it easy for them.

One more thing. Employers and recruiters often look for candidates on social networking sites, so be sure to have a page on the largest sites—and on any other site where they might be looking for someone like you.

Once you're registered on one or more social networking sites and have invited your current network to connect with you, you can use those sites to make your job hunting more effective.

SOCIAL NETWORKING SITES ARE A NETWORKING TOOL

Some career-oriented social networking sites allow you to send an e-mail to everyone in your entire network who works in a certain organization. I think that's the right idea. Contacting people at your targets is exactly what you want to do. But I don't like that way of doing it. It's too impersonal to be highly effective networking. Doing that kind of mass e-mail contact is a little too close to spam. You're moving into the cool zone when you don't need to.

Instead, try it like this. Use your social networking sites to locate people who are inside your target organizations or worked there in the past. If you already know them, you can contact them directly, by e-mail or phone. But wait—don't do it yet. First take the next step.

Use your social networking sites to find people you don't know who are current Insiders or former employees at your targeted organizations. Then look to see which of your contacts know them. You may find, for example, that Rob, an Inner Circle contact you've known for years, once worked at Target A. Maybe you also discover that three people on Rob's list of contacts now work at your Targets B, C, and D.

Now you have three topics you want to talk to Rob about: what he knows about A, those three people he knows that work at B, C, and D, and what else he might know that relates to your Target List and job search. What you're doing here is using the social networking site to help you map networks and discover connections.

Next, you talk to Rob real time, on the phone or in person. Maybe you e-mail him first, but the real time conversation is the most likely to be productive. You cover all three topics, including them in a single networking conversation like those we discussed in Chapter Seven on meetings with personal contacts. And, of course, you find out what else he knows.

It's important for you to talk to Rob about his contacts at B, C, and D before you contact them. Don't just send them an e-mail, even if the Website will do that for you. You want to know how well Rob knows those three. He may not know them at all. Or he may know them but not like them very much. Ask him.

You also want to know whether Rob thinks it would be a good idea for you to talk to them. If he knows the two of you, he'll have a good guess about whether the conversation will work. If he thinks it's a good idea, you want to find out more about them so you know where to go—and not go—in your conversation with them. And, if he's comfortable doing so, you want Rob to introduce you. Or at least you want his permission to use his name.

The designers of Websites sometimes want you to believe that everything can be done by clicking buttons on the sites. But it can't. Computers are superb at searching and organizing information. They can be a great help to you that way. But you need to do your own communication. In job hunting, it usually works better if it is personal, not impersonal. And it certainly works better when it doesn't look anything like mass mailings or spam.

The other reason it's important for you to have conversations—not just e-mail—with people is about expectations and job openings. As we discussed in Chapters Two and Three, when people hear that you're looking for a job, they think first about job openings and who's hiring. They often believe that you want information only on those two topics. They may believe that the only way they can help you is by telling you where the openings are or by introducing you to the mythical Mr. Bigshot. Sometimes it takes some explanation to get them re-focused on what you really need.

So, while it may be slower than sending out a whole pile of e-mails all at once, it's also much more effective to talk to people the old fashioned way, one at a time. I'm not saying to never send out a group e-mail. It might be smart to do that sometimes. But I am definitely saying, don't blow it with your best contacts. Treat them like they're important. They are.

Using social networking sites to locate inside contacts at your targets and to locate the people who can connect you with them is a big time-saver. It also lets you better prioritize your work, choosing the most promising opportunities and working on them first.

If you have a hundred or more "connections" or "friends" on a social networking site and each of them has a hundred, you have access to a lot of people at the second and third degrees of separation. Don't even think about trying to use all of them. Select those where your odds look best.

There's another way social networking sites can speed your job hunt. When you're looking at your friend Marc's page, browse through his contacts. If the site allows it, look at their pages. Look for people with whom you might have things in common. Networking, as you recall, is all about common interests. If you share personal or professional interests with any of Marc's contacts, these might also be people you'd want to meet—even if there is not an obvious, direct connection with your Target List.

Note the names of these people and check them out with Marc. Point out the listed common interests, and ask Marc if he thinks you and that person might enjoy meeting each other. If he says yes, then do as we discussed in Chapter Seven on personal contacts. Get acquainted and see where it goes. You've got nothing to lose. If you don't get any job-hunting information, maybe you'll at least find a new tennis partner.

You may remember that one of the myths in Chapter Three was "A networking group is the only place to network." Let's take a look and see whether networking groups might be useful for you. And at the best ways to use them, if they are.

Making the Most of Networking Groups

Pick the best one for you.

Take your Target List.

Don't try to get everything done at the meeting.

Focus on information, not job openings.

Employment-related networking groups are often held in churches and synagogues. Sometimes they are for members of that organization only. More commonly, they are open to any job hunter who wants to attend. Some incorporate religious practices into the networking meetings. Some do not. If you're a member of a religious community that has such a group, you should certainly try it. And of course, networking groups are also held in other venues, such as libraries or community organizations.

The meeting designs, as we discussed in Chapter Three are sometimes loosely structured and sometimes more organized. Some have trainings or talks on various aspects of job hunting. These talks are sometimes given by well-meaning amateurs who don't give very good advice. And sometimes they are given by highly experienced experts, people you would have to pay $100 an hour or more to hire.

So the first step is to see if you can find one that you like. If you do, you may decide to attend regularly. With the right people and the right meeting design, it can be highly beneficial to your search.

Whatever the design of the networking group, there are things you can do to make it more effective for you. First, bring multiple copies of your Target List as well as your resume and possibly business cards. Some groups are set up to exchange resumes between all other members. That can be a useful way to locate the right contacts. Exchanging Target Lists can be even better.

But exchanging paperwork is only one step. You should arrange future get-togethers with some of the people you meet. Giving them copies of your resume and Target Lists gets the next meeting off to a faster start.

Business cards can be useful even for unemployed people, because they're a convenient way of giving someone your phone number and e-mail address. If you're employed, be careful about giving out your current employer's card in a job search.

It's smart to plan and practice a brief statement of the kinds of work you're looking for and your related qualifications—your Professional Objective and Core Message. Some groups ask all participants to introduce themselves this way in two minutes. Or one. Even if they don't ask, you'll want to use a statement like this with most of the people you talk to. It's part of getting your message out.

It's even smarter to add the names of three or four of your local targeted employers to that kind of introduction. Build it into your introduction, or tag it onto the end, like this:

"The employers I'm most interested in are _____, _____, *and* _____ . *I don't know if they're hiring right now, but I figure that sooner or later they will be, so I'm pursuing them. If you know anything at all about any of those organizations—or organizations like them—I'd really like to talk to you before we leave."*

Job hunters sometimes decline to go to these networking groups because "they're just a bunch of unemployed people complaining about how tough job hunting is." The complaining part can sometimes be a problem, but unemployed people are also people with networks and information. You might want to work at the company that just let one of them go.

So as usual, what's most useful at networking groups are conversations about your targeted organizations and people who know about them. You're looking for people who might have information and are willing to share it. Or another way is even simpler: you're looking for people you're comfortable talking to.

It's usually smarter at a large meeting to look for a number of people that you can talk to in depth later, rather than spending your time talking to one person in depth at the meeting.

So talk about your targets, and encourage others to do the same. When you see possibilities for mutual assistance, set up a coffee date. At the outset, an in-person meeting is usually better than on the phone, because networking is easier when you get to know each other. If you find one person you want to talk with more, you and that person might together select another two and put together a foursome for lunch. Then you can all look for ways to help each other with information about targets and possibly introductions.

Don't forget to ask people in the large networking group to introduce you to others in the group. And do the same if you can: introduce people you meet to people you already know. It helps everyone, including you.

Some of these networking groups put an inordinate focus on job listings, sometimes even asking participants to bring in lists of job openings. As I've said, I think this is a less productive activity. Part of your job at that kind of meeting might be to shift the focus of discussion from where the openings are to what your targets are.

SOME NETWORKING GROUPS DO NOT INCLUDE ANY NETWORKING

Here is the most important thing I have to say about networking groups: sometimes they're not about networking at all. Some are entirely in the cool zone. Or completely cold.

If you don't know anyone in the group and have no pre-existing connection with other participants, what you're doing is actually not networking it all. It's more like sales. Unless you're very outgoing, highly confident, and have some selling skills, job hunting this way is difficult.

It's only in those groups where you already know some of the people—or have an organizational connection with all of them—that you're actually doing networking from the beginning. In others, you're starting cold. However, if the group meets weekly and you attend regularly, you will discover connections, build relationships, and, through time, shift into real networking.

There's another networking strategy that's not used by everyone, but important to people with a large or distant personal job market. It can be particularly important for people in executive or other high level positions where their personal job market includes more than one geographic area.

Out of Town and International Networking

Make a Target List for your planned relocation city.
Use your hometown contacts to reach people in your targeted city.
Look for useful organizational contacts in your hometown.
Visit if possible.

I'll talk about this as if you were considering only one distant city. It works the same if you have more than one out-of-town target city in mind, and because networks are global, the principles are the same for international networking.

First, create your Target List for the city you want to move to, and start talking to any personal or Level Three professional contacts you have in that city about that list. This can be by e-mail and phone. Ask them for referrals. Even if you start with only one or two people, your network there can expand significantly if they're willing to actively help.

Show your Target List to hometown contacts as well, making it clear where the targets are. In your discussions, ask everyone if they know anyone at all in your targeted city who they'd be willing to introduce you to. You'll also ask about your targets, of course. But if you're moving to Omaha, then another critical question is *"Do you know anyone in Omaha?"* And the follow-up is, *"Do you know anyone who might know someone in Omaha?"*

Ask your hometown contacts if they'd be comfortable asking around for you to try to locate additional contacts in your city of destination.

You want general information on the city you're considering, so anyone at all who lives there is a good starting point. When you're talking to them, you can also ask them to look at your Target List. And you can ask for introductions to other local people.

The main point is to make good use of your hometown contacts. Until you explicitly ask them, you don't know what kind of contacts they have in your target city. So I'd suggest talking extensively to your hometown network and anyone else you know, regardless of where they live.

These days, people know other people all over the world. Someone you know in a third city—or even in another country—could have friends in your target city that they never mentioned because the subject never came up. So talk to all of your personal contacts, regardless of where they live.

Check to see if any of the organizations on your Target List have facilities in both cities. If so, start with the hometown facility. See if

Insiders there will introduce you to people in their organization in the target city.

If you're a member of any organizations that have members in both cities, work through that as well. This could include professional organizations, alumni groups, churches, synagogues, and many others. These organizational connections are sometimes the key to success in an out-of-town search. Again, use your Target List with members in both cities.

Some of those organizations are also communities. You should always look for communities where you can network in your city of destination. This works for international networking as well. For example, a native of India looking for a job in the United States should see if they can find someone to introduce them into an Indian-American community in the United States. An American looking for a job in Paris should look for introductions into an American ex-pat community there.

If you're able to make a trip to visit the target city, see if you can actually meet some people you haven't yet met. Sometimes the (honest) line, *"I'll be in town for only three days"* will help you get appointments with Insiders or even Decision Makers, assuming of course that you have an introduction.

I think it's also very important to tell people—especially in the targeted city—that you're definitely planning a relocation. Some job hunters even "borrow" a local address from a friend to use on the resume, because an out-of-town street address may put employers off. A cell phone number, of course works anywhere, as does an e-mail address.

Whether you're looking out of town or only near your current residence, you may want to consider consulting.

The Consulting Strategy

If people with your work background sometimes act as paid consultants to organizations, you may want to consider doing that yourself.

It's not uncommon for unemployed managers and executives—as well as mid- to upper-level professionals in many fields—to do consulting while networking for a new job.

It works like this. You define the consulting practice, something you'd honestly be good at. You print business cards and maybe put up a Web page. You get your first consulting gig from a friend, possibly at a reduced rate. As soon as you have one consulting engagement, you're not unemployed. You're a consultant.

It can make professional networking easier by taking the issue of your unemployment off the table. You can look for a job and for consulting work at the same time. If enough consulting comes in, maybe you'll give up the idea of finding a job. On the other hand, if you're talking to someone about a consulting assignment, and it looks like it might be better for both of you if you worked for them as an employee, well, you could give up the consulting, couldn't you? It's a good strategy, because you win either way.

A variation of the consulting strategy is project work or temp work. It's not just about administrative assistants these days. Many professional and managerial jobs are also included, right up to—no kidding—temporary CEO.

If your planned job search is particularly difficult for any reason, or might take longer than average, this strategy is especially worth considering. Or if you're in a job search that has inadvertently taken too long already, it can remove the stigma of being unemployed too long. And, yes, you could maybe bring in some income while job hunting.

Combine Networking With the Other Six Search Techniques

Although networking is the single most effective job search technique for the majority of people, it's only one of seven interview-getting activities. The other six are walking-in, direct mail, cold calling, applications, ads and postings, and recruiters and staffing firms. These six are all effective, at least sometimes, for some people.

So before we wrap up this chapter, I want to remind you of them and suggest that you consider including some of them of in your job-hunting activities. I want you to do whatever works in your job search, as long as it is honest and won't damage your reputation. Often the best way to find out if a technique works for you is to try it. If, like checking the Internet job boards, it doesn't take much time or cost any money, why not try?

The "informal" or networking approach to job search is how 50 to 75 percent of job hunters find new jobs. The other six formal job-search techniques do work for some job hunters. If you go this way, you'll usually meet the Decision Maker only if you pass some initial screening and become a finalist candidate.

The two main formal job-search techniques are using recruiters and responding to ads or Internet postings. Most experts agree that these two formal techniques are how 25 to 50 percent of job hunters find new jobs. When using both of these methods, you are going after jobs that have been announced as currently open. In both cases, there is significant competition, because the jobs are known to be open, so these techniques are reactive, not proactive. In both cases, it's all about your resume, and not about who you are as a person—at least not on the first screening.

Resumes submitted for advertised jobs are usually entered into a database. Employers or recruiters then search the database using key-words. Naturally, the most common keywords used are job titles. A recruiter looking for candidates for a CEO position will surely look for people who have already held that title, president, or some other similar title. This is not surprising, because a recruiter can collect a $200,000 fee for filling a $600,000 CEO position. Someone paying that kind of money expects to see candidates already proven success-ful in a very similar job.

The same is true of employers searching a database of resumes submitted for any job. Although it certainly does not cost $200,000 per person, employers do pay a fee to hire an employment agency to locate mid-level candidates or to get the privilege of searching an online job board's database.

Again, the most obvious keyword to use is the job title. If that job title is not on your resume, then you're not listed in the results of the keyword search. Of course, an employer may use other keywords. They might also search for keywords that describe skills essential to the job. In looking for a computer programmer, for example, an employer would probably use the name of a programming language as a keyword. In other occupations where central skills can be identified, they are also used as keywords. But job titles are the easiest and most obvious way to go, aren't they?

If the employer or recruiter comes up with a nice long list of resumes of people who have already held the desired job title, an obvious way to narrow the search is to use the names of the most prestigious employers in the field. So if you haven't yet held the "right" titles with the "right" companies or don't have the "right" skills on your resume, it's less likely that these formal job-search techniques will work for you. You are probably among the 50 to 75 percent of job hunters who will find their jobs through networking.

Someone looking for a recent grad will probably favor certain colleges and universities and certain majors, using corresponding key words. And they might search GPAs, because that's another easy way to go.

If you don't have a top GPA from a top university, welcome to the real world. By definition, 50 percent of graduates are in the bottom half of the class. But, hey, don't worry. After a few years, they look at your work experience and stop asking about your GPA. But without the "right" keywords right now, your resume will not come up in database searches. Then you're also among the 50 to 75 percent of job hunters who will find their job through networking.

On the other hand, if you have a strong resume showing the kind of work experience and job titles that your Target Market is looking for, your chances in this formal job market are good. Want to know for sure if recruiters and the Internet job boards will work for you? Try them. But get started networking while you're doing that.

The other four techniques, walking-in, direct mail, cold calling, and applications are all in the cold category, out there beyond the cool zone. Walking in is about presenting yourself in person—without an appointment—at the targeted employer. It works well for some hourly jobs and a few entry-level professional jobs as well, but it's very time consuming.

Applications are a variation of walking in. They're less time consuming because you can usually do them online, without actually walking anywhere. But again, they're most appropriate for hourly and some entry-level jobs. If you're looking for a government job, applications will be important and you should use networking to learn how to complete them correctly. For most other salaried jobs, you will complete the application only after they decide to hire you—if at all.

The last two, cold calling and direct mail, both involve making contact with total strangers, people who have never heard of you— without an introduction. Most job hunters do use these now and then, but using them as your primary techniques is probably not a good idea, because both require a very large number of contacts and telemarketing also requires a thick skin.

When using either of these, do what ever you can to warm them up. Any common interest or introduction—even a weak one—helps considerably. Your odds go up considerably when you make them a little more like networking.

TRY ALL OF THE OTHER SIX TECHNIQUES—AND KEEP NETWORKING

Keep working on your networking while you try these other methods. It's probably smart to begin your search with networking only, to make sure you've gotten some feedback on your plans and that you're on the right track. And, as we've said, networking will help you make the most of other techniques by providing the information you need to make good decisions.

That's the last of the seven tools and strategies that can make effective job-search networking even more effective. I hope you found some ideas you can put to work in your job hunting.

We have now completed the "Decide-Prepare-Talk" parts of the Decide-Prepare-Talk-Land sequence. The next chapter is about the landing-a-job part. If you have a good Search Plan and stick with it—working on it every week—you *will* land a job.

In the meantime, stay with the talking. It's the one most important thing you can do in your search. So do it well and do it persistently. Talk about the good things you can do for your next employer. And talk about how very interested you are in a particular group of organizations, those on your Target List.

Don't skip the last chapter. The part about follow-up with Decision Makers is one of the most important things in this book. Doing it will shorten your search.

ORVILLE'S JOURNAL

Job Hunting, Tibet, Suze, and the Pool Table

I hadn't seen Ben for a while, not even to shoot a little pool. But now Ben, Jessie, and I were having lunch in the Tibetan restaurant. He was finishing up a yak meat dish. I was still working on my lentil soup and a steamed roll. Jessie ate her last mo-mo and got the conversation going again.

"You know, Orville, Ben's job search has been going really well since he got over his thing about not asking anyone for help."

"He listens to you now?"

"Yes, it was just a week or two at the beginning where it was a problem."

Ben pushed his empty plate to the side. "Since then, it's been all about 'I Get By With a Little Help from My Friends,'" he said, singing the song title.

Jessie turned to look at him. "How do you know all those '50s songs?"

"They're not '50s," Ben replied. "The Beatles weren't even born in the '50s. They were born in the late '80's, like you, hon."

"Yes," she said, smiling and looking at the huge mural of Lhasa, "and they were born in Tibet, just like me. Tell Orville about your three lunches."

"Good idea. Orville, it's all finally paying off. Or at least it's getting close to the payoff. In the last two weeks, I had three lunches with Decision Makers. None of them is admitting to having an opening, but all three are high on my Target List."

He turned to Jessie and stage-whispered, "Now watch, Orville's going to say, 'Good. What else.'"

"Good." I said. "What else?" I can take a hint.

"I'm glad you asked. I've now met and talked to 18 different Decision Makers. That's a daggone lot of networking." He pointed at me, cueing me.

"Good. What else?" Sometimes my job is easy.

"I've answered a total of 32 Internet ads and got two callbacks. No interviews yet."

"That's about par for that course," I said, departing from my script. "What else?"

"Miles introduced me to three people. When we had lunch." He looked at Jessie. "After I apologized for the Super Bowl thing."

Now that's amazing. Totally awesome," I said. "On both sides."

"And I've had two interviews. One job turned out to pay less than my last one. The other one was 500 miles from here. The job and pay were both okay but not great. And 500 miles is too far."

"This is all good. Excellent, even," I said. "Can we go back to the three lunches?"

"Sure."

"I like that they're all companies high on your Target List. This was all through networking? Tell me about them."

"Yes, networking. One was a regional manager from a consulting company. The other two were both manufacturers. One is a short commute, over on the western edge of town. The other would be a relocation, but only about 100 miles. Nobody's talked about a specific job, but I've

checked them out and they all have a reputation for paying well."

"The pay is important." Jessie got back into the conversation. "We've been reading about money management
since Ben's been unemployed. In case his severance ran
out."

"Good move." I had suggested that to Ben at the beginning. I was glad to hear they'd done it. You never know
how long a search might take.

"We checked out Suze Orman," Ben added, "and we
got to thinking about money long term as well as short
term. We're doing pretty well, all in all. We got out of
debt about four years ago. But Suze and the other books
all said the same thing. We're not doing well enough on
savings."

"So compensation is high on your list?" I asked.

"Yes."

"That suggests consulting. Or being open to a bigger
relocation."

"Yes, I know. I'm looking more carefully at consulting. Alicia's friend got me started."

"Good."

"Look Jessie, Orville said 'Good' without saying 'What
else?' I finally got a break."

"I'm happy for you to have a break now and then, as
long as you don't slack off for more than one day a week."

Jessie looked to see if I was kidding. I wasn't. She
looked back at Ben. "He's really tough, isn't he?"

"Yes," Ben put in, "I'm going to be really happy when
I have a new job so I can throttle back and get some
breathing room."

"Ben, you're doing just fine." I said. "You've been working hard. And you're running a great search. If it goes on much longer, you'll be as good a networker as Rachel. But you really had me worried for a minute there."

"Worried? How?" He looked puzzled.

"Well, when you were talking about your financial situation..." I paused.

"What?"

"For one terrible minute, I thought you were going to say you were selling the pool table."

And then you get the offer…

| DECIDE | PREPARE | TALK | LAND |

Chapter Ten

Moving From Networking to Interviews and Job Offers

Sometimes people say that they are "networking for a job." I understand what they mean, but no one really networks for a job. You network to get the message out. You network to gather information. Networking is a great way to meet some new people, including Decision Makers. It's networking that gets you to the right place at the right time with the right information.

Then you're close. You're in the endgame. It's a time when you need to go beyond networking You have just a few more things to do in order to convert the opportunities you locate by networking into an actual job. The first of these is persistent follow-up with the Decision Maker.

Follow-Up, Follow-Up, Follow-Up

Once you have succeeded in making contact with the Decision Maker in a targeted organization it's very important that you stay in touch with that person on a regular basis. Unless they create a position for you (that *does* happen sometimes), you are now essentially waiting for the next opening. Because you arrived before the opening, there isn't a crowd of competing candidates. With a little bit of luck, you are the only candidate who is actually on the scene and asking to be the next person hired.

Of course you are doing this in more than one organization. When you are in touch with enough different Decision Makers in enough different organizations, the odds tip in your favor, and one of them has an opening. Because you talked to a number of Decision Makers, it's not an accident that one of them now has an opening. And it's because of your attention to follow-up that you're on their short list.

Follow-up with Decision Makers is one of the most important things you'll do in a job search. This isn't about networking. It's what happens at the end of the networking process and before you get the interview.

Once you have talked to an appropriate Decision Maker, you should re-contact that person every two or three weeks until they hire you. Or until someone else hires you. How often you make contact depends on how highly paid the job is. In higher paying jobs, every three weeks is usually about right. In lower paid jobs, you should make contact more often.

Lee Hecht Harrison once did a study on this. We found that the most effective job hunters, the ones who get jobs more quickly, did a great deal more follow-up with Decision Makers. Those who neglected follow-up with Decision Makers had longer job searches.

When I ask job hunters why they don't do this kind of Decision Maker follow-up, they usually say, "I don't want to bother them." But you'd have to ask, "what do you have to lose?" It looks to me like you could lose the opportunity by not continuing to make contact. And if you do continue to make follow-up contacts in appropriate ways, you'll be seen as highly interested rather than bothersome.

If that's not entirely clear, imagine that you are the Decision Maker. A candidate proactively approaches you and tells you how very interested they are in working for you. Then many weeks pass and you never hear from them again. What would you think?

Most Decision Makers would think that the candidate found another job. Or maybe that the candidate wasn't really as interested as they said they were. Either way, they're likely to cross you off the list of potential employees. Or simply forget about you. Then all that work you did in networking to make contact with the Decision Maker is wasted.

DID I MENTION FOLLOW-UP?

Meeting a Decision Maker by networking is a major victory in job search. So when you succeed with that, please do your follow-up. Stay with it, even if they are not encouraging you. Keep on telling them how very interested you are. Here are some examples of what you can say in voice mails, notes, e-mails, and phone calls.

I saw that great article about you in yesterday's Gazette. Congratulations. It reminded me of all the reasons that I'd like to work for a company like yours.

I was over at Geiser Corp yesterday and met Samantha Shuster. She said to say hello to you. We were discussing some of the same operational issues you and I discussed. She had some great insights that I'd like to share with you the next time we talk.

I've been busy with several consulting assignments lately but I thought I'd take a minute to let you know that I'm still very interested in that job we discussed. If it looks like the budget for it is close to approval I'd like to stop by and tell you and your team why I think I'd be a great choice for it.

I came across an Internet posting about the product designs you mentioned when I last saw you. I thought you might be interested, so here's the link: _____. I continue to be very enthusiastic about joining your company the next time an opportunity arises.

This is just a quick note to let you know that I'm more interested than ever in working in your department the next time you need someone.

Exactly what you say isn't as important as the fact that you're keeping your name in front of them, and letting them know that you're still interested and still available. You can and should do this with other Insiders as well as with Decision Makers.

The more Decision Makers you are following up with, the more likely it is that one of them will want to have you come in for a formal interview next week.

NETWORKING, INTERVIEWING, AND DECISION MAKERS

Networking, then, is how you get into the right organization. It's how you get the chance to talk to the right Decision Maker. Once you get there, you do persistent follow up and set your sights on actually getting the next appropriate job to come open.

In order to get the job, you need to convince a Decision Maker that you're a good choice. If you have been networking effectively, you have been disseminating positive information about yourself. With a little bit of luck, some of that positive information about you has already gotten to the Decision Maker. If so, it will help you with the interview.

When you have networked your way into an organization, interviewing is usually easier. The Decision Maker is more likely to see you as a known quantity. This is particularly true when you have been introduced to the Decision Maker by someone they know and trust. Being introduced by another Insider—someone who has the Decision Maker's ear—is a common way this happens.

If all of this sounds like I am suggesting that you make every effort to prejudice the Decision Maker in your favor before the interview, that's exactly correct. After all, once you have connected with Insiders, your most important job is advocacy. If you took a case to court, you would have a lawyer advocating your cause, arguing for you. In job search you need to do that for yourself.

Interviews and Offers

In the interview itself, your research and your knowledge of the organization and the job pay dividends again. When preparing for the interview, you will go back and review the files that you have been building on this target organization. Based on what you know, you can better focus what you say at the interview. You can also ask better questions.

After the interview and before the offer, you have the opportunity to continue advocating for yourself. Of course you will do that in a written communication with the Decision Maker immediately after the interview. But if you networked into the organization, you may also have the opportunity to "send messages" through other people about your continuing strong interest.

If you were lucky enough to find a sponsor inside the organization, you may also be able to get information about the decision-making process as it is happening. Of course, you should also make post-interview follow-up arrangements with the Decision Maker— setting a time when you will contact them to see how things are going and whether they need anything more from you.

Once you have an offer, negotiating it is sometimes easier when you have networked in. It can make the process friendlier. But please don't let that distract you from your job in negotiation. You may still need to ask for what's fair and reasonable—and perhaps a little more than that.

Starting a New Job

When you got there by networking, starting a new job can also be easier. You already know some Insiders. Now you can continue to build relationships with them. You got off to a good start with the Decision Maker, who is now your boss. You already have good information about the organization. You're off to a good start in a new job.

But you've got one more thing to do to wrap up your job-search networking.

Remember to Say Thank You

Thank everyone.

Tell them you were successful.

Give them the name of your new organization and your job title.

When you've succeeded in your search, don't forget to say thank you to all the people with whom you networked. Of course, this is the polite thing to do, maybe the kind of thing your mother taught you. And it's the right thing to do. But it's more than that.

It's also good career management. If you found a job by networking, you probably talked to a lot of people. They heard the beginning of the story, how you were looking for the right work in the right organization. Now they should also hear the happy ending. Don't leave them hanging. Let them know that you were successful. Give them credit for their parts in your success. Express your gratitude.

These thank-yous are most powerful when they're specific and personal. You may want to go back to your records of your search and see who helped with what. When you thank Steve for the two introductions that netted information that led to your job, that will mean more to him than a more general "thanks for all your help."

You've probably noticed that I've been suggesting personal e-mails and phone calls in many networking situations. This is another one where that advice is applicable. With your personal contacts, I'd suggest a phone call or personal e-mail to each one. In some cases, you might want to consider a small token gift of some kind, along with a hand written note.

With your professional contacts, the thank-you is important in the same way. And it's equally important to let all of them know exactly where you landed, your new organization, and your new job title. This will tell them exactly how successful you were. It will also let them know where to find you, which opens the door to the kind of continued professional networking that can help both of you do your jobs better. And might also help you both find your next jobs more easily, when that day comes.

It's a good idea to get your new business card into the hands of all of your professional contacts, because that's a concrete reminder that makes it more likely that they'll remember where to find you. Sending an e-mail from your new business e-mail address is also useful, because it makes it easy for them to get you into their address book.

The problem with doing these follow-up activities is that you're likely to be unusually busy in the first 90 days of your new job. So prepare the mailing in advance, then put your business card in it later and send it off.

Before you start your new job, while you still have time, you can also call or e-mail your professional contacts. Then the business card or the e-mail from your new address is a simple follow-up. And your transition is complete.

MOST JOB HUNTERS FIND JOBS BY NETWORKING. YOU CAN TOO.

I said at the beginning that I would be as complete as possible in talking to you about how networking works in a job search. I've done that, and I hope I've given you what you need to succeed.

For most people, networking takes some experimentation as they learn it. It also takes some time and some perseverance—and more of those in difficult economic times than in good times. But most people also find that a networking search builds momentum as you get the hang of it.

One thing I know for sure is that someone who wants to find a job and is willing to work on it can find one. During the last 30 years, I've seen that thousands of times. So work hard, and more importantly, work smart on your job search. Hang in there. Don't give up.

With a little bit of luck, you will not need to do everything I talked about in this book. In fact, you may very well find a new job when you're just getting started on following some of this advice. If so, I'll hope you won't be too disappointed that you didn't get a chance to try all of it.

May you find a great new job.

May you soon be shaking the boss's hand and agreeing on a starting date.

May you enjoy your new job and prosper in it.

ORVILLE'S JOURNAL

We Celebrate Ben's Success With ARM

It was a really nice restaurant. Pink tablecloths. Fresh flowers. Candles. A maitre d'. It was already worth the 45-minute drive it took to get there.

Judy, Rachel, and Jessie were having an animated conversation, with Ben and I bringing up the rear. We were seated in a small private room. Ben had special-ordered vegetarian entrées for Judy and me. We ordered the rest of the meal, then Ben tapped on his glass and cleared his throat ostentatiously.

"Ladies and gentlemen, as a newly appointed Vice President of ARM Consulting, I would like to welcome you to this celebration."

"Hear, hear." Rachel said, as we all applauded politely.

"ARM Consulting?" asked Judy, "What's that? Medical care?"

"Well, that's my next speech," Ben said. "A-R-M is Automation, Robotics, Manufacturing. We do consulting on production lines and software, of course, but also on the hydraulic, pneumatic, and electro-mechanical arms..."

"Ben..." Jessie gently interrupted him.

"Yes?"

"How about skipping the technical stuff and telling us about your great new job?"

"But that wasn't technical. That was the layman's version."

Jessie turned to Judy. "Is Orville like that? Or is it just Ben?"

Judy smiled. "Well, he's not geeky. But don't ask about

careers or job hunting unless you're interested in a serious conversation."

"I'm glad you found something more technical than managerial, Ben." The waiter was serving my appetizer. A delicate sculpture of cheese and vegetables.

"And I'm glad you found something that pays a ton of money," Jessie added.

"Me too," Rachel put in, "I don't always get invited to places like this."

"I thought you didn't want consulting." Judy was admiring her stuffed mushrooms. Also a work of art.

"I was concerned about the travel," Ben explained, "but the money is really good. It's 165 percent of my old salary, plus bonus. And I get paid for solving really interesting engineering problems."

"What about the travel?" Rachel asked. "Are we ever going to see you? Or will you just be stopping in once a year to take us to the best restaurants in the state?"

"It turns out that there are only about 82 days a year when I don't sleep at home," Ben said. "The company is putting hi-def videoconferencing in our house, so a lot of the work will come to me. And I can actually see hi def shots of what's happening with a production line anywhere."

"It sounds like a great job and a great office set-up," I put in. "How about telling us about the networking part. How did you get this job?"

"The networking worked like a great production line. I talked to Rachel. She introduced me to Alicia. Alica introduced me to a former engineering professor who is now a full time consultant. He told me about ARM." Ben took a forkful of his appetizer, some kind of baked fruit.

"It sounded interesting, so I checked it out on the Internet. Then I went through my contacts and found a passive contact—a guy who graduated from my college—who worked there. That's where I got the inside scoop. The pay. The travel. The home office set up."

"Then Rachel found a physics professor at Walcott who actually knew the Decision Maker at ARM." Ben raised his wine glass in Rachel's direction. Thank you Rachel."

"And, Judy, thank you too." He looked back at me. "Did you know Judy made two introductions for me?"

"Yes, I heard."

Jessie turned to Rachel. "Did you know Judy's my career coach? For education. In about four years, I'm going to become an elementary school teacher."

"You're giving up business?"

"Yes, right around the time that Ben stops this consulting stuff. We'll be way ahead on our savings by then."

"Yes," said Ben, "Still miles away from retirement, but maybe ready for a different kind of career. Right now, though, I need to finish my thank-you's."

We all looked his way. He was getting ready for another speech.

"Alicia couldn't make it tonight," Ben added, "so I sent her a gift certificate for two so she could come here another time."

"Maybe she'll want to bring one of her dear friends from The Wall." Jessie said, looking at Rachel.

"And, Jess," Ben turned to his wife, "I couldn't have made it without you. Thanks hon."

The waiters were clearing the appetizers and serving the main course. Ben turned to me.

"Orville, I want you to know that we are not only keeping the pool table, we have added amenities. I thought maybe you might want to play sometimes while Judy and Jessie are visiting with each other."

"I can play even when you're out of town? Thanks, Ben. What are the amenities?"

"Jessie and I are now the proud owners of the world's only pool room with a pear, apple, and grape cooler and a complete jasmine tea setup with Yin Hao, Dragon Pearl, the whole thing. This networking stuff really works. Thanks, Orville."

Index

About the Author

Orville Pierson is the author of *The Unwritten Rules of the Highly Effective Job Search*, a book that has enjoyed wide acceptance by executives, mid-level managers, and professionals of all kinds. It has also been included in career programs at Duke, DePaul, Mount Holyoke, and Purdue, to name a few—and featured at an alumni event at the Harvard Business School.

Mr. Pierson is also senior vice president, corporate director of program design and service delivery for Lee Hecht Harrison, a leading career services company with 240 offices worldwide. His work there includes creating books, Websites, and videos on career management for the firm's private clients, who number up to 100,000 a year. Since 1977, he has trained hundreds of career consultants for several different career services firms.

Yale educated, Mr. Pierson is in demand as a speaker for college events, church and synagogue career programs and job hunters ranging from entry-level to senior executives. Often quoted by journalists, he was selected as a job hunting expert by ABC News Primetime and his work has been repeatedly featured on radio and TV.